Analyzing Discourse:
A Manual of Basic Concepts

Volume Editor

Bonnie Brown

Production Staff

Bonnie Brown, Managing Editor
Karoline Fisher, Compositor
Hazel Shorey, Graphic Artist

Analyzing Discourse:
A Manual of Basic Concepts

Robert A. Dooley
and
Stephen H. Levinsohn

A Publication of
SIL International
Dallas, Texas

Copies of this and other publications of SIL International may be obtained
from

International Academic Bookstore
SIL International
7500 W. Camp Wisdom Road
Dallas, TX 75236-5699

Voice: 972-708-7404
Fax: 972-708-7363
Email: academic_books@sil.org
Internet: http://www.sil.org

Contents

Preface

This manual has been written as an introduction to discourse analysis for future linguistic field workers. We believe that the most effective way for most people to learn how discourse works in a particular language is by interacting with discourse principles while analyzing texts from that language. We therefore present the essential minimum, the most basic concepts of discourse, as a foundation for subsequent in-depth analysis with field data. We also believe that basic discourse notions are invaluable in all aspects of a language program. Those aspects range from language learning to lexical, semantic, and morphosyntactic analysis, right on through to linguistic applications such as education and literature production, where clear communication is of fundamental importance.

Our goals for this manual imply a combination of features that we have not found elsewhere. First, we intend it to be practical, addressing issues commonly confronted by field linguists. Rather than attempting to apply a rigid theory or survey a variety of approaches, we provide a methodology that has been refined over years of use. Second, although we follow no rigid theory, we aim for more than a "grab bag" of diverse methodologies by attempting to present the material within a coherent and productive framework. Specifically, we follow a functional and cognitive approach that seems to be a good approximation of how discourse is actually produced and understood. Third, we have kept the manual brief. Most chapters are no longer than six pages, and the whole can be covered in fifteen classroom hours. Although our aim is introductory rather than comprehensive, we do provide references for further reading on the topics discussed.

The manual can be used individually or in group sessions, such as in a formal course or a working seminar (linguistic workshop). In a group setting, concepts can be illustrated by examining further texts, from a single language, language area, family or type, or from a typological variety of languages.

Our grateful thanks go to all those who have given us feedback on the contents of this manual, pointing out errors and suggesting how the chapters could be improved. We would like particularly to mention Paul Vollrath, who worked through every chapter in depth and put a lot of thought into how the material could more clearly be presented.

Chapters 1–4

Types of Text

1

Means of Production: Number of Speakers

In natural language, sentences are typically found in discourses, just as words are typically found in sentences. But what constitutes a discourse? How are discourses organized? Most speakers have only a vague idea.

One of the reasons for this vagueness is that there are many different types of discourse, and each type exhibits characteristic kinds of organization. So, before we address the question of how discourses are alike in later parts of this manual, here we survey a few of the dimensions along which they can differ. Specifically, in this chapter we take note of discourse features "which tend to remain stable over fairly long stretches" and, often, for an entire discourse, as opposed to "features which tend to undergo continuing change and modification during discourse" (Leech 1983:12). It is these stable features of discourse which allow us to speak of "types of text".[1]

1.1 Discourse dimensions

Discourses typically differ along a number of dimensions, which include the following:

- the means of production: the number of speakers who produced the discourse (chapter 1);
- the type of content: the text genre (chapter 2);

---

[1]In this manual, the two terms *discourse* and *text* can generally be taken as synonymous. An overview of the current field of discourse studies is found in Van Dijk 1997; a history of the field is given in de Beaugrande 1997.

- the manner of production: style and register (chapter 3); and
- the medium of production: oral versus written (chapter 4).

As will become apparent, any classification of discourse along such a small number of dimensions does not do justice to the variety that is actually found. For one thing, each of the four dimensions mentioned above could yield a much richer division than will be attempted here. For another, discourses of any one type can be found embedded in discourses of another; several degrees of embedding are common (see section 2.2).

1.2 Monologue versus dialogue

One of the dimensions along which discourses differ involves the number of speakers involved in their production. Some discourses are produced by a single speaker; these are referred to as MONOLOGUES. Other discourses are produced by more than one speaker; these are referred to as DIALOGUES or CONVERSATIONS.[2] This manual will be concerned principally with monologue, so section 1.3 makes a few observations about dialogue.[3]

1.3 Conversational turns and moves in dialogue

What a given speaker says in a dialogue before another one speaks is referred to as a CONVERSATIONAL TURN. Example (1) is part of a dialogue and involves three conversational turns: two by speaker A and one by speaker B:

(1)   A: Can you tell me why you eat all that food?
       B: To keep you strong.
       A: To keep you strong, yes, to keep you strong.
          Why do you want to be strong?

Within a turn, there may be different functional MOVES. In (1), for example, speaker A's second utterance has one turn, but two moves (Coulthard 1977:69): an evaluation of speaker B's utterance *(To keep you strong, yes, to keep you strong)* and a further question *(Why do you want to be strong?)*.

Longacre (1996, chapter 5) identifies different kinds of moves (he calls them utterances). First, there is an INITIATING MOVE (IM), which begins a dialogic exchange. This exchange is in some sense terminated, or given closure, by means of a RESOLVING MOVE (RM). In (1), for example, both questions

---

[2]In this manual, the term *speaker* will be used of the person who originates the discourse (whether in speech or in writing), and *hearer* will be used of the person who receives it.

[3]What we call monologue is often jointly produced to some extent: for example, "narratives are authored not only by those who introduce them but also by the many readers and interlocutors who influence the direction of the narrative" (Ochs 1997:185).

posed by speaker A—*Can you tell me why you eat all that food?* and *Why do you want to be strong?*—are <u>initiating moves</u>. In turn, speaker B's answer to A's first question,—*To keep you strong*—is a <u>resolving move</u> which terminates the exchange. The first two conversational turns of (1) may, therefore, be labeled as follows:

(2)   A: Can you tell me why you eat all that food? (IM)
        B: To keep you strong. (RM)

Whatever else may be found in the dialogue of which (2) is a part, (2) itself forms a recognizable unit, or chunk, of discourse. Chunks occur in all types of discourse, and we will examine them later in more general terms. Here we simply observe that in dialogue we often find a characteristic kind of chunk, which begins with an initiating move and ends with a corresponding resolving move. This chunk is sometimes called an adjacency pair (Coulthard 1977:70—see also section 14.2), although, as we shall see, the two parts may not actually be adjacent.

Longacre identifies another type of move in dialogue: a countering move (CM), which, coming between the initiating move and the corresponding resolving move, <u>delays the resolution or closure</u>.[4] At times, a countering move may have a second function, as an initiating move in its own right, and in consequence may give rise to its own resolving move. This is seen in the following dialogue chunk (Longacre 1996:132f). Three countering moves represent new initiatives, which result in four levels of resolution (the indentation indicates relevant pairings of initiating moves and resolving moves):

(3)   A: I'm inviting you to dinner with me at 2 P.M. Thursday (IM)
        B: Can I bring one of my sons? (CM/IM)
            A: Bob or Bill? (CM/IM)
                B: Does it matter which? (CM/IM)
            A: Yes, it certainly matters. (RM)
        B: Okay, Bob, the older one. (RM)
      A: Very well. (RM)
    B: Okay, thanks, we'll be there. (RM)

Of course, not all dialogues have such symmetrical closure. In (4), for instance (Longacre 1996:131), what the final utterance resolves (to use the term loosely) is A's immediately preceding utterance; A's original initiating move remains unresolved, as does B's continuing/initiating move:

---

[4]Longacre's term is "continuing utterance".

(4)   A: Where are you going, Bob? (IM)
            B: Why do you want to know? (CM/IM)
                A: You always get mad like this. (CM/IM)
            B: Liar! (RM)

Notions such as initiating, resolving, and countering moves are helpful in analyzing dialogue. Often, however, things are more complicated than this.

- Conversations do not always take place in neat "turns". Even in American English, with its norm of only one person speaking at any given time, there are sometimes "gaps" (when no one is speaking) and "overlaps" (when more than one person is speaking) (Coulthard 1977:53). Some cultures routinely allow simultaneous speakers, so that participants are both speakers and hearers at the same time.

- Cultures also have different ways to indicate that a speaker's turn has ended or come to a "possible completion". Signals of this can be grammatical (e.g., the end of a utterance), paralinguistic (e.g., loudness, rate of speech), or kinesic (eye contact, hand motions, etc.) (Coulthard 1977:52–62). Another culture-specific set of norms deals with who can speak when.

- Three categories of conversational moves (initiating, countering, and resolving moves) may not be adequate, as Longacre himself notes. For example, the first move of A's second turn in (1) appears not to fit into any of these categories.

Key Concepts:
monologue
dialogue/conversation
   conversational turn
   move
      adjacency pair
         initiating move
         resolving move
      countering move

2

Type of Content: Text Genres

For a given language and culture, many texts fall into recognizable types. As English is used in America, for example, the business letter and the brief greeting exchange between two busy people are distinctive types. Each text type has a particular social or cultural purpose, around which clusters a characteristic combination of linguistic or textual properties. These textual properties often include a typical number of speakers (usually one or two), a certain register, and a particular medium of production (all of which are discussed in these introductory chapters). Additional characteristics may be a certain limited range of content and a distinctive overall structure or formal constraints of other kinds, as lines for poetry. The types of text which can be characterized in this way, as recognizable combinations of textual properties in pursuit of a particular cultural goal, are called GENRES (Bakhtin 1986:60; Eggins and Martin 1997:236); Longacre (1996:8) uses the term *notional type.*

A large part of the analysis that is done on discourse can only be genre-specific. Although business letters and greeting exchanges will have certain elements in common simply because both are discourses, many linguistic observations about a given text cannot be generalized; they only hold for the specific type. "The linguist who ignores discourse typology can only come to grief" (Longacre 1996:7).

2.1 Broad categories of genre

By definition then, genre is culture-specific, and each language and culture will have a bewildering variety of specific genres which are

7

distinctive to it.[5] Hence, any list of universal genres must be more general. In this text, a very broad level of genre categories is presented, following Longacre 1996. Not surprisingly, these general categories lack many of the characteristic properties associated with specific genres; they do, however, retain useful distinctives.

Longacre's broad categorization makes use of plus and minus values for a set of four features. Two of these features—contingent temporal succession and agent orientation—can be taken as primary, and serve to identify the four broadest categories. CONTINGENT TEMPORAL SUCCESSION refers to a framework "in which some (often most) of the events or doings are contingent on previous events or doings" (p. 9). Thus, Little Red Riding Hood's arrival at her grandmother's house is contingent on her setting out through the woods, and the putting of a cake in the oven (in a recipe) is contingent on having first mixed the proper ingredients. The second primary feature, AGENT ORIENTATION, refers to whether the discourse type deals with "events or doings" which are controlled by an agent (one who performs an action), "with at least a partial identity of agent reference running through the discourse" (loc. cit.). Again, Little Red Riding Hood and the wolf are agents in that story; the hearer is a (potential) agent in an exhortation, etc.

The four categories of genre resulting from these two features are presented in (5):

(5)   Broad categories of genre (from Longacre 1996, chapter 1)

		Agent orientation	
		+	−
Contingent temporal succession	+	Narrative	Procedural
	−	Behavioral	Expository

That is, NARRATIVE discourse (e.g., stories) is + agent orientation + contingent succession for the reasons discussed above. PROCEDURAL discourse ("how to do it, how it was done, how it takes place") is + contingent succession but − agent orientation, since "attention is on what is done or made, not on who does it" (loc. cit.). BEHAVIORAL discourse (exhortation, eulogy, some speeches of political candidates, etc.) is − contingent succession but + agent orientation, since "it deals with how people

---

[5]According to Bakhtin (1986:80), "no list of oral speech genres yet exists, or even a principle on which such a list might be based."

did or should behave" (loc. cit.), and EXPOSITORY discourse (budgets, scientific articles, etc.) is – in regard to both features.

Besides these two primary features, Longacre discusses two further ones: projection and tension. PROJECTION in its + value "has to do with a situation or action which is contemplated, enjoined, or anticipated, but not realized"; prophecy is + projection narrative, stories are – projection, and so forth (p. 9, but cf. 9.4 in this manual). TENSION "has to do with whether a discourse reflects a struggle or polarization of some sort". Narrative can be + or – tension, as can scientific articles (depending on how polemic they are), etc. (p. 10). For beginning discourse analysis, narrative texts with + tension and two or three main participants are recommended.

Longacre's classification of broad genres is based primarily on content. More specific genres often involve other textual properties. Drama, for example, may be a narrative according to broad genre, but one which is presented in the form of dialogue (chapter 1) and is typically written (chapter 4) for live presentation. Letters are written discourses and may be of any one of several genres. Jokes are typically oral narratives with a particular goal (humor) and a specific register of speech, and so forth.

2.2 Embedding and communicative intent

As was mentioned in chapter 1, discourses can be, and often are, embedded in other discourses. Dialogue can be embedded in monologue (as often happens in a novel), narrative can be embedded in behavioral discourse (e.g., an illustration in a sermon), and so on. This kind of embedding may involve several levels.

The fact of embedding complicates the classification of texts. Is a fable a special kind of narrative with a moral added at the end, or is it a behavioral discourse with an embedded narrative (which happens to account for most of its length)? A similar question can be asked in regard to parables with an application appended. And what of a parable, say, in which the moral or application is not given explicitly, but is only implied? Some analysts would classify it according to its form (as a narrative), while others would classify it by its function (as a behavioral text), in which case the embedded narrative accounts for 100 percent of its actual length!

Questions of text classification, as above, often involve the speaker's intent, the reasons why the text was produced. As we have seen, genres themselves have characteristic purposes or functions within the culture. Some genres have a fairly specific function: brief greeting exchanges to maintain social relations in a minimal way, and behavioral texts to influence the addressee's behavior or attitudes. The cultural function of other genres, such as narrative as a broad genre, is more vague. In addition to the established cultural goal for a genre, the speaker usually has individual goals that are context-specific. The combination of purposes underlying a text is called the speaker's COMMUNICATIVE INTENT. "People aren't just telling stories (or talking) for no good reason, but they're offering something of an interactional nature that *does* something such as describing or explaining or accounting for the 'current circumstances' in some way" (Spielman 1981:14). Communicative intent is diverse and generally layered (Nuyts 1991:52). A narrative, for example, might be told with the intent of entertaining the hearer, but with a less obvious intent of solidifying one's reputation as a storyteller, and so forth. The choice of genre itself has communicative intent: Why would my boss give me just a brief greeting exchange this morning rather than being more chatty? The question of intent is not, at bottom, a purely linguistic one, although it can be reflected linguistically. It's a broader question, involving the reasons that lie behind actions in general.

A text type, then, is a culturally-typical type of action which is performed by linguistic means. Communicative intent has to do with reasons that lie behind the linguistic action.

Key Concepts:
genre
  primary features
    contingent temporal succession
    agent orientation
  broad classification
    narrative
    procedural
    behavioral
    expository
embedded discourse
communicative intent

3

Manner of Production: Style and Register

Style and register both have to do with choices that speakers make in using language. STYLE looks at individual speaker preferences or speech habits, while REGISTER deals with how an entire speech community typically uses language differently in different situations (Eggins and Martin 1997:234).

3.1 Individual style

When the same story is told by different speakers, differences typically show up. Even when the speakers include the same content, they package things in different ways.

Lyons (1977(2):614) uses the term INDIVIDUAL STYLE to refer to "those features of a text...which identify it as being the product of a particular author" [or speaker] and which represent his or her choice as regards manner of expression. Thus, we can contrast the style of Hemingway and Dickens in literary texts, or of language associates Juan and Pedro in field work.[6]

There is a further complexity: a speaker is not limited to a single style. For one thing, it is typical for a new writer, whether in a neoliterate society or not, to evolve a written style over a certain period of time, thus, in effect, changing styles. For another, a speaker may be experimenting, for

---

[6]Sandig and Selting 1997 provide a useful overview of the study of discourse styles.

whatever reason, with different styles for similar discourse tasks. Still, an association of style with a speaker is generally useful.

This does not mean that a speaker will "sound the same" on every occasion. In the following discussion of register, it will be apparent that different occasions predictably give rise to different manners of expression. Rather, individual style can be thought of as the pattern of how a speaker will typically express him or herself, given a certain set of circumstances and text type.

One simple, common difference of individual style concerns sentence-initial connectives (e.g., expressions like 'because of that', 'after that', 'so', etc.). The choice and frequency of such elements is subject to a variety of factors, of which genre is one and individual style is another. In a given genre, some speakers may typically be quite sparing with such elements, while others are liberal with them. Similarly, one speaker will typically have a certain set of connectives that he or she employs according to a characteristic pattern, while another has a different set and/or a different pattern. When discourse analysis is done on the basis of a very limited number of texts, individual style must be kept in mind in drawing conclusions.

3.2 Register

Halliday (1978:31f) uses the term REGISTER to refer "to the fact that the language we speak or write varies according to the type of situation", that is, according to "the social context of language use". At least two dimensions of register are relevant: the type of transaction that is taking place between speaker and hearer (which Halliday calls *field*), and the interpersonal relationship which holds between them (which he calls *tenor*).[7]

Consider the following excerpt from a business letter (Howell and Memering 1986:383):

---

[7]Halliday (1978:33) includes one other heading under register: node (channel, mode). In this manual, this is dealt with separately; see chapter 4.

(6)

> Lawrence Masterson
> 907 High Road, Apt. 12
> Emmy, Michigan 48902
> January 9, 1986
>
> Mr. Clay Torrence
> Emtor Sports, Inc.
> 134 159th Avenue
> New York, New York 10112
>
> Dear Mr. Torrence:
>
> For Christmas I received from a distant relative a "Home Tension-Stress Meter", model number 18956, made by Emtor Sports, Inc.
>
> The meter worked only once....
>
> ...I am writing to you for assistance. Should the meter be sent to you, or is there a customer service center where I could send it for repair or replacement?
>
> Yours,
> Lawrence Masterson

The fact that (6) is a letter implies certain things as to overall form (heading, greeting, closing, signature). Beyond this, it has several features that relate to register. First, as regards field, the fact that it is a business transaction is reflected in choices of vocabulary (*assistance* rather than *help, repair* instead of *fixing,* etc.) and of the information presented (e.g., the model number of the meter, but not its shape). Second, as regards tenor, the writer presents himself as one who is not personally acquainted with the addressee; this comes out in such things as the form of address *(Mr. Torrence)* and the lack of chatty personal information (e.g., how the weather has been in Michigan).

In many contexts, the speaker-hearer axis is quite prominent. Ritual versus everyday situations (field) and deference versus exercise of power (tenor) are common but striking differences of register.

3.3 A note on genre

Register can often be predicted from genre: the register of a business letter, for example, is different from that of a casual exchange or joke. Individual style is somewhat different in this regard. In some genres, the range of individual style does indeed tend to be rigidly constrained, as in business letters and military commands, which have standard forms. For other genres, however, such as "artistic" or "literary" types, the display of personal expression, hence of individual style, is a major function (Bakhtin 1986:63).

3.4 A note on dialect

Since style and register deal with aspects of language over which the speaker exercises choice, they have traditionally been distinguished from dialect (e.g., Halliday 1978:33–35). However, this distinction can only hold if the speaker truly exercises no choice in regard to dialect. Recent studies of code switching (including dialect switching) bring to light very common situations in which speakers do have options in regard to language or dialect, and in which they exercise those options in coherent and purposeful ways. "If, for example, the standard dialect is used in formal contexts and the neighbourhood one in informal contexts", dialect is being used as an expression of register (Halliday 1978:34; see also Lyons 1977(2):617f).

Key Concepts:
style
register
how these concepts are related to genre and dialect

4

Medium of Production: Oral Versus Written

This chapter summarizes the most common differences that have been observed between oral and written texts *of the same genre.* Such differences show up, for instance, when comparing oral and written versions of a narrative given by an accomplished storyteller, or when comparing recorded and printed versions of a political address. As Bartsch says (1997:45), "Different genres have different features, and it is not helpful to compare oranges to apples." Consequently, comparisons between oral texts of one genre and written texts of another may be misleading (see Chafe 1985b for a comparison between dinner table conversation and academic prose which falls into this trap).

Bartsch's article not only compares an oral and a written version of the same narrative in an Algonquian language of North America, but also includes a useful bibliography of recent publications on variations between speech and writing.

4.1 Frequency of repetition

"Spoken language uses a lot of repetition. But in written language there is a limit to how much repetition can be tolerated by readers" (Aaron 1998:3). Bartsch's comparison of the oral and written forms of an Algonquian story revealed that the same teaching point was made four or five times in the oral version, but only once in the written one. Similarly, if a reported speech was longer than one sentence, the SPEECH ORIENTER (e.g., *he said,* sometimes called "quotation margin", "quote tag", etc.) was often repeated in the oral version, but not in the written one.

A distinctive form of repetition frequently found in oral material is TAIL-HEAD LINKAGE (Thompson and Longacre 1985:209–213). This consists of the repetition in a subordinate clause, at the beginning (the "head") of a new sentence, of at least the main verb of the previous sentence (the "tail"),[8] as in...*he arrived at the house. **When he arrived at the house,** he saw a snake.* Johnston (1976:66) found that tail-head linkage, considered the "life blood of narrative discourse in most Papua New Guinea languages", was edited out of written texts by native speakers.

In oral texts in some languages, EVIDENTIALS (or "verification markers", such as 'witnessed', 'hearsay', or 'deduced', which indicate the source of evidence of the information being presented—see Barnes 1984 and Palmer 1986) occur in every sentence. In written texts, however, once the source of the information has been established, evidentials tend to be used only sparingly.

4.2 Deviations from default orders

Variations from the default or unmarked order of constituents in clauses or sentences are more frequent in oral than in written material. This is because spoken utterances are accompanied by intonation contours that unite constituents into larger units, and by pauses that help to signal boundaries between units. Such variations may be less acceptable in written material. For instance, Chafe (1985b:115) observes that antitopics in English *(Never been to a wedding dance. **Neither of us.)** tend to be used only in oral material.

In the Inga (Quechuan) language of Colombia, the default position of the verb is at the end of its clause. In oral material, it is common for the verb to be followed by nominal or adverbial constituents, and for main clauses to be followed by subordinate ones. When such texts were written down and read aloud, however, native speakers invariably ended sentences with the main verb and began a new sentence with the material that followed it, even though the punctuation indicated that the sentence concerned had not ended.

4.3 Organization

Written style is more concise and better organized, and introduces new information at a faster pace (Chafe 1992:268). Bartsch found that purpose

---

[8]Neither "head" nor "tail" is used here in a common linguistic sense. In particular, "head" does not refer to grammatical head, and "tail" does not refer to the entity to be discussed under that name in chapter 11.

clauses were much more frequent in the written form of the Algonquian story than in the oral version. Conversely, the oral version had "more author intrusions, extra explanatory material that wasn't part of the story line" (1997:45).

Groupings of sentences tend to be longer in written than in oral material. For example, oral material tends to organize reported speech in pairings of initiating moves and resolving moves (see chapter 1), whereas written material tends to be organized into larger groupings (Levinsohn 2000:218–219).

4.4 Preciseness

Because writers have more time to think of "the right word" than speakers, written text is characterized by more careful word choice than even the most carefully planned oral material (Biber 1988:163). In contrast, spoken language often uses HEDGES (Lakoff 1972) like *sort of* and *kind of*, as in *He started sort of circling* (Chafe 1985b:121).

Chafe (p. 114) also notes that the English lexicon consists of three kinds of items: COLLOQUIAL VOCABULARY that is used predominantly in speaking (e.g., *guy, stuff, scary*), LITERARY VOCABULARY that is used predominantly in writing (e.g., *display, heed*), and VOCABULARY THAT IS NEUTRAL with respect to this distinction (neutral equivalents of the above colloquial and literary words are *man, material, frightening, show, pay attention to*).

4.5 Paralinguistic signals

"Spoken language relies heavily on prosody (pitch, pause, tempo, voice quality, etc.) and body language for deixis, respect, interpropositional relations, and a host of other categories" (Aaron 1998:3). Written language relies on punctuation and description to convey similar effects, but generally in an under-coded manner.

Certain deictics, such as indefinite *this* in English (*I woke up with **this** headache*), may also be restricted to oral material (Chafe 1985b:115).

4.6 Practical applications

Differences between oral and written language have specific applicability to many types of practical linguistic work.

In language teaching (including ESL), for example, we note that the range of skills needed by new readers only partially overlaps with those needed by new speakers. In regard to vernacular literacy, Nida (1967:156) notes, "in languages with a very short literacy tradition, e.g., those in which people have written for only twenty or thirty years [or two or three], certain significant differences of written and oral style rapidly emerge. Accordingly, one cannot set down as a criterion of good written style...merely the oral style of good speakers..." This has broad implications for reading materials of all types, including translation (which, according to Bartsch, may need to combine features of oral as well as written texts).

Nevertheless, it is becoming clear that the oral versus written dichotomy is probably an amalgam of different parameters that can be teased apart (see Biber 1988). Therefore, in field linguistics one needs to collect as many types of texts as possible and label them, not simply as oral or written, but with detailed circumstances of their production.[9]

Key Concepts:
repetition
    speech orienters
    tail-head linkage
    evidentials
deviations from default orders
organization
    explanations
preciseness
    hedges
    colloquial vocabulary
    literary vocabulary
    neutral vocabulary
paralinguistic signals

---

[9]For other articles on characteristic features of oral and written modes of language, see Frank 1983.

Chapters 5–15

Common Characteristics in Discourses

5

Coherence

My view of physics is that you make discoveries but, in a certain sense, you never really understand them. You learn how to manipulate them, but you never really understand them. "Understanding" would mean relating them to something else—to something more profound....(physicist I. I. Rabi, *The New Yorker*, October 20, 1975, p. 96)

Chapters 1–4 discussed text types, or how discourses differ. We now begin to consider things that discourses of all types have in common.

The organization that hearers associate with a discourse is not simply a matter of the linguistic structure that appears. Rather, on a more fundamental level, it is a reflection of how the content comes together and is stored in the mind. The forms of language that the speaker uses certainly play a part in this, but psychological research shows that the way hearers understand, store, and remember a discourse corresponds only partially with what was actually said.[10] Other things that go into the hearers' MENTAL REPRESENTATION of a discourse are their prior knowledge of the way things happen in the real world and their expectations of what the speaker means to say. Obviously, this prior knowledge and expectation is based heavily on culture-specific experience. Hearers may bring as much to their understanding of a discourse as they get from what the speaker actually says; "discourses...force us to draw upon all we know about our culture, language, and world" (Everett 1992:19).

---

[10]See, for example, Paivio and Begg 1981:194 ("research shows that we remember the gist of what was said better than we remember how it was said") and the references they provide.

To understand mental representations, we need to know more than discourse content plus cultural knowledge and expectations. We also need to recognize some general processes of human cognition, e.g., how people perceive, store, and access information. Although these processes may not be directly observable, they are reflected in how discourse is put together and how that organization is signalled.[11] In this text, mental representations and related psychological notions will serve as a major theme integrating the discussion. In return for this, they will be expected to "pay their way" by helping explain what we find in actual language data.

As a first step in this direction, we consider what it means for a discourse to be coherent.

5.1 Coherence

"What is discourse? What is it that makes a sequence of sentences into a coherent whole as opposed to a chaotic assemblage?" Johnson-Laird (1983:356) asks these questions and then provides two examples:

(7)   It was the Christmas party at Heighton that was one of the turning points in Perkins' life. The duchess had sent him a three-page wire in the hyperbolic style of her class, conveying a vague impression that she and the Duke had arranged to commit suicide together if Perkins didn't "chuck" any previous engagement he had made. And Perkins had felt in a slipshod sort of way—for at that period he was incapable of ordered thought—he might as well be at Heighton as anywhere....

(8)   The baying of the hounds and the screaming of the chickens echoed below me, as I quickly scanned the tracks leading towards the hole—this was going to be a hectic breakfast. I thought I'd better eat a full meal because of the task ahead and the difficulties I might encounter. But it was only when I had cooked myself a steak, and that piece of shark meat that had been ignored by everyone, that I discovered that I could

---

[11]See Johnson-Laird 1983, chapter 14 and Paivio and Begg 1981, chapter 4, as well as Chafe's (1991:356) statement, "discourse cannot be understood apart from its psychological and social factors". An overview of cognition in discourse studies is found in Graesser et al. 1997. Unfortunately, there is no consensus on "the basic 'shape' or format of conceptual representation: theories range from...propositional or proposition-like systems—no doubt the most frequent view—to image-based systems, over types of mixed systems combining proposition-like and image-like representations, and abstract systems..." (Pederson and Nuyts 1997:2).

> only pick at these tidbits, having, as I now recalled, break-
> fasted, lunched and dined to repletion already. Rather than
> throw the food away, I rang up my husband at work and
> asked him to bring home some colleagues to dine with us.

If you are a typical text interpreter, you recognized that (7) deals with a consistent cluster of concepts, even though it is only a text fragment and you may never have experienced what it describes (Johnson-Laird cites this passage from *Perkins and Mankind* by Max Beerbohm). Your mental representation of (7) might include such things as the following:

(9)   a. a place called Heighton (otherwise unknown to you?)
      b. a Christmas party (and your expectations of what that
         might involve)
      c. a male (probably adult) named Perkins
      d. a duchess (and your expectations about nobility) who
         knows Perkins and expresses herself somewhat flamboyantly
      e. an invitation from the duchess to Perkins to come to the
         party, etc.

By constructing a mental representation which included such elements, you probably came to accept (7) as (a fragment of) a coherent text.

You may have initially assumed that you would also be able to construct a mental representation for (8). As you tried to follow it, however, your idea of what it was talking about probably became difficult to maintain: what kind of home could have below it "the baying of the hounds and the screaming of the chickens"?; was the meal to be eaten actually breakfast, or some meal later in the day?; etc. So, at some point you probably gave up constructing a mental representation for (8) with any confidence. At that point, (8) ceased to be coherent for you.[12]

A text is said to be COHERENT if, for a certain hearer on a certain hearing/reading, he or she is able to fit its different elements into a single overall mental representation.[13] When a text fails to cohere, the hearer in

---

[12](8) was not designed to be coherent, at least in an overall sense. A different person composed each sentence, and each person only knew of the immediately preceding sentence.

[13]See Johnson-Laird 1983:370: "a necessary and sufficient condition for a discourse to be coherent, as opposed to a random sequence of sentences, is that it is possible to construct a single mental model from it". Johnson-Laird uses the term *mental model* in a specific way, as a technical term with respect to his theory. In the present manual, the term *mental representation*, which owes much to Johnson-Laird and others, is not used in a technical sense, but can be thought of as roughly meaning "conceptual framework". The structure of mental representations is discussed further in chapter 9.

essence says, "I'm unable to construct an overall mental representation for it at this time."

Coherence is often spoken of as if it were a property of a text; more precisely, though, it concerns what a certain hearer is able to do with the text at a certain time. This allows a single text to cohere for some hearers but not for others, as often happens when there are differences in culture or other background. Alternatively, in the case of a single hearer, it allows a text to fail to cohere at one time but cohere later on, or cohere initially and stop cohering when certain new material is added. Having made this point, however, we will still sometimes speak of coherence as a property of a text, but with the understanding that that is a derivative notion, a prediction that typical attempts at finding a coherent interpretation will be successful.

A text comes with the presumption of coherence: that is, if a speaker is presenting something as a text, the hearer is entitled to assume that it will yield a coherent interpretation and will direct his or her efforts accordingly (Brown and Yule 1983:199; Halliday and Hasan 1976:54).[14] If you processed (7) as coherent, and if you tried to process (8) as coherent, then you were acting on this presumption, which is foundational to successful communication.

A mental representation for a text does not generally come full-blown into the hearer's mind. Rather, it is shaped in successive stages by trial and error. In the initial stages of the text, the hearer posits a tentative representation for it.[15] Then he or she amplifies and modifies that representation, updating it as the discourse unfolds, so that each item of information is accomodated in a plausible way.

5.2 Context and contextualization

The notion of context has already been referred to. The CONTEXT for something is the situation in which it is embedded, in which it is seen as a part of a larger whole. Since, for our purposes, the only important kind of context is context that one is aware of, context can be thought of in terms of mental

---

[14]On the level of individual utterances, Sperber and Wilson speak of the "presumption of relevance" (1986:156ff). In grammar, constructions presumably come with some presumption of parsibility. These are probably special cases of a more general presumption of processability, which would hold for genuine acts of communication of any size.

[15]Sometimes the speaker leads the hearer through this process systematically, introducing time, location, main participants, props, etc., in orderly sequence. This can give rise to formulaic openings: "Once upon a time, in the land of X, there lived a Y." In other texts, the speaker, as it were, tosses the hearer bodily into the middle of the story, and the hearer's efforts to deduce an adequate mental representation become a point of interest in following it.

representations: the part of one's mental representation which is connected to or surrounds the concept in question. Fillmore (1981) uses the term CONTEXTUALIZATION to talk about the hearer's progressive attempt to develop a viable mental representation for a text. For a given text and a given hearer, two kinds of contextualization take place, often simultaneously: internal and external. In INTERNAL CONTEXTUALIZATION, the hearer attempts to construct a mental representation for the content of the text itself. In this manual, we will follow the common practice of calling the hearer's text-internal representation his or her TEXT WORLD.[16] In EXTERNAL CONTEXTUALIZATION, the hearer tries to understand what the speaker is trying to accomplish by producing the text (i.e., the speaker's communicative intent; see section 2.2). It is the real-world context for the text, a mental representation in which the text world is embedded, and thus includes the speaker, hearer(s), and all circumstances that are relevant to the purpose of the text.

In our earlier discussion of (7) and (8), we focused on internal contextualization, i.e., whether what was being described "made sense". (9) is a partial internal contextualization (text world) for (7). For (8), you probably found no single text world that accommodated all the information in any obvious way. For these two examples, along with trying to work out an internal contextualization, you were doubtless also working on external contextualization. You probably recognized that (7) was being presented to you as an example of a coherent text, and you may or may not have initially assumed the same for (8). However, when an internal contextualization for (8) kept failing—when it began to prove difficult, if not impossible, to come up with a text world for it—you likely came up with an external contextualization of it which said that (8) was being presented as an example of noncoherence. If so, then for you (8) had a viable external contextualization, even though it lacked an internal one; in fact, your difficulty in coming up with an internal contextualization was what led you to an external one!

Key Concepts:
mental representation
coherence
    internal contextualization
        text world
    external contextualization

---

[16]Other terms sometimes used for this kind of mental representation are *macrostructure* (van Dijk 1977) and *textual world* (de Beaugrande and Dressler 1981).

6

Cohesion

In chapter 5 we saw that the coherence of a text is, in essence, a question of whether the hearer can make it "hang together" conceptually, that is, interpret it within a single mental representation. Does the fact that coherence is a conceptual phenomenon mean that linguistic signals are irrelevant to it? Not at all. On the contrary, the speaker will plant linguistic signals in the text as clues to assist the hearers in coming up with an adequate mental representation.

This phenomenon is called COHESION, and can be defined briefly as the use of linguistic means to signal coherence (see Grimes 1975:112ff; Halliday and Hasan 1976; de Beaugrande and Dressler 1981:3; Brown and Yule 1983:191ff). Signals of cohesion indicate how the part of the text with which they occur links up conceptually with some other part. It is common to speak of such signals as COHESIVE TIES.

In the present chapter, several types of cohesive ties are discussed and illustrated. Each language will, of course, have its own range of devices which can be used for cohesion, but some general types will be found cross-linguistically. The following list in (10) is taken largely from a well-known treatment of cohesion by Halliday and Hasan (1976), as amplified by Brown and Yule (1983, section 6.1).

(10)   Common types of cohesion

    Descriptive expressions alluding to entities mentioned earlier

    Identity
      repetition (whole or partial)
      lexical replacement
      pronouns
      other pro-forms
      substitution
      ellipsis

    Lexical relations
      hyponymy (type of)
      part-whole
      collocation

    Morphosyntactic patterns
      consistency of inflectional categories (tense, aspect,
      etc.)
      echoic utterances
      discourse-pragmatic structuring

    Signals of relations between propositions

    Intonation patterns

These types of cohesion are illustrated briefly in turn. Many of the following examples are taken from Brown and Yule 1983.

6.1 Descriptive expressions alluding to entities mentioned earlier

Perhaps the most obvious kind of cohesion consists of DESCRIPTIVE EXPRESSIONS such as *the following day, in the next room,* and *the girl's brother.* Such expressions allude to entities that were mentioned earlier in the text, or at least to entities that the speaker assumes the hearer already has in his or her mental representation.[17] For the expressions listed above, the earlier entities could be the preceding day, a certain room, and the girl. The cohesion lies in the fact that the new entity is explicitly linked to the earlier entity, thus contributing to coherence.

Some of the following types of cohesion overlap with descriptive expressions.

---

[17]See section 9.3 for discussion of the term *entity*.

6.2 Identity

Cohesive ties under the broad heading of IDENTITY link to identical forms, identical meaning, or identical reference or denotation.

In REPETITION, an entire expression (as in (11)), or at least a recognizable part of it (as in (12)), is repeated.

(11)   **The Prime Minister** recorded her thanks to the Foreign Secretary. **The Prime Minister** was most eloquent.

(12)   **Dr. E. C. R. Reeve** chaired the meeting. **Dr. Reeve** invited Mr. Phillips to report on the state of the gardens.

In LEXICAL REPLACEMENT, the forms in question differ, but the referent or denotation is the same:

(13)   **Ro's daughter** is ill again. **The child** is hardly ever well.

An expression such as *the child* will be successful in referring to Ro's daughter if, at that point, the accessible part of the hearer's mental representation contains just one entity which this expression fits (taking into account also what is said about the child). Similar comments hold about any definite referring expression (see section 10.2).

PRONOUNS also involve identity of reference (i.e., coreference), generally without identity of form.

(14)   **Ro** said **she** would have to take Sophie to the doctor.

There are other kinds of PRO-FORMS besides pronouns. Pro-verbs are one type, such as *do...it* (Halliday and Hasan 1976:126).

(15)   I told someone to **feed the cat.** Has **it** been **done**?

Halliday and Hasan (1976:88) use the term SUBSTITUTION for a kind of partial identity of denotation: two things are of the same type, but are different instances (tokens) of that type.

(16)   Jules has **a birthday** next month. Elspeth has **one** too.

ELLIPSIS can be thought of as either coreference by means of zero or "substitution by zero" (Halliday and Hasan 1976:143).[18] Coreferential ellipsis is represented by ∅ in (17).

(17)   **Jules** has a birthday next month and ∅ is planning a big celebration.

The substitution type of ellipsis is illustrated by (18).

(18)   Hans is **a freshman.** I am ∅ too.

6.3 Lexical relations

Many pairs of lexical items are related in ways that do not involve identity. Three such lexical relations are illustrated here.

In HYPONYMY, one thing is a subtype of another. For example, daffodils are a subtype of flower; *daffodil* is a hyponym of *flower.*

(19)   **Flowers** have always been interesting to me. **Daffodils** are my favorite.

Another important relationship is the PART-WHOLE one.

(20)   **The human body** is an intricate mechanism. **The arm,** for example, is used for different kinds of leverage.

COLLOCATION is "the habitual co-occurrence of individual lexical items" (Crystal 1997:69), e.g., by virtue of belonging to the same lexical set.

(21)   **Monday** is not my favorite day. **Tuesday** is only slightly better.

6.4 Morphosyntactic patterns

Morphosyntactic patterns also offer many opportunities for cohesion. Three types of patterns are illustrated here.

First, a sequence of clauses and sentences can show CONSISTENCY/IDENTITY OF INFLECTIONAL CATEGORIES, e.g., tense marking, as in (22).

---

[18]More precisely, according to Halliday and Hasan (1976:144), "ellipsis occurs when something that is structurally necessary is left unsaid". Elided material must be, in some sense, informationally given so as to be recoverable, and in general cannot be the main point (focus) of the utterance. For these notions, see chapters 10 and 11.

(22)   The jumper **landed** sideways on the slope. The right ski **snapped** just in front of the boot.

The fact that the two verbs in (22) have simple past tense suggests that they are both events within the main narrative sequence.

Second, a kind of morphosyntactic repetition, whole or in part, is found in ECHOIC UTTERANCES. An echoic utterance is one which copies all or part of an earlier utterance, and it is obvious that the speaker intends it to do so. The echoic utterance calls attention back to the earlier utterance in order to imply a comment about it. (23) is an example from Sperber and Wilson (1986:237–43).

(23)   Speaker A: **It's a lovely day for a picnic.**
       Speaker B: **It's lovely day for a picnic,** indeed.

In (23), speaker B's utterance is echoic and could be understood perhaps as ironic of the preceding utterance, e.g., if the day is rainy, or as in agreement with it, if the day is nice. Whatever the interpretation of an echoic utterance may be—contextual clues are needed—it makes reference to the earlier utterance, thus forging a cohesive tie.

Third, cohesion in morphosyntactic patterns includes what in chapter 11 will be described as DISCOURSE-PRAGMATIC STRUCTURING. Of the patterns of this type, only one is illustrated here: POINT OF DEPARTURE PLUS PREDICATION, as illustrated from the translation of the beginning of a text in Mbyá Guaraní of Brazil in (24).

(24)   a. **Long ago,** there were two houses.
       b. **In one of them** lived a newlywed.
       c. **In one** lived his father-in-law.

Points of departure (the bolded expressions in (24a–c)) serve to link the following predication to something that the hearer is assumed to have already in his or her mental representation. The expression *long ago* in (24a), for instance, references a time frame which is grounded in the present.

6.5 Signals of relations between propositions

A general principle in human language is Behaghel's Law, which states, "items that belong together mentally are grouped together syntactically" (MacWhinney 1991:276). One application of Behaghel's Law is that, when two sentences are adjacent, or two clauses are adjacent within a sentence, then, other things being equal, the propositions they embody should be interpreted as being in a close conceptual relation. (Other things that may not be equal would include a signaled break of some kind between the two.) Thus, juxtaposition can suggest cohesion, even though by itself it does not signal a specific conceptual relation.

Conceptual (semantic) relations between propositions are sometimes referred to as COHERENCE RELATIONS. At times these are rendered explicitly by conjunctions or other linguistic markers. This is the case in (25), which is taken from a computer software brochure:

(25)   For the first time, you can display Help and work on your
       document at the same time. **For example,** you could display
       and read the procedure for creating a glossary entry at the
       same time you create one in your document.

In (25), the expression *for example* may not be strictly necessary so that the hearer/reader can come up with a coherent interpretation linking the sentences, but it makes the intended interpretation easier and surer (see chapter 13).

6.6 Intonation patterns

Although an adequate treatment of intonation in discourse is beyond the scope of this manual, the importance of intonation as a cohesive device should not be underestimated. One can often tell from intonation alone when a speaker is "winding down" his or her talk. That involves cohesion, since it places an utterance within the overall scheme (e.g., near the end) of the discourse. On a more local scale, parenthetical information is often signaled by means of a low-key intonation pattern (Cruttenden 1986:129, from which the following example is taken).

(26)   Well I saw Jim the other day // **incidentally / he's just got
       married again** // and he said...

Parenthetical information, by definition, stands in a certain relationship with surrounding material, so that any signal of it is cohesion.

6.7 How important is cohesion?

Since coherence is a matter of conceptual unity and cohesion is linguistic form, it is in principle possible to have coherence without cohesion.

Brown and Yule (1983:196) claim that it is "easy to find texts, in the sense of contiguous sentences which we readily co-interpret, which display few, if any, explicit markers of cohesive relations". They furnish (27), from a letter from a literary agent, as an example.

(27)   Just to test the water I made one telephone call yesterday, to a leading British publisher with offices in New York. There was immediate interest in *Clear Speech.*

Brown and Yule's claim uses a rather odd notion of text ("contiguous sentences"); (27) is that, but is not an entire text in the common usage of the term. This is important: a fuller context could well bring to light cohesive ties between (27) and the rest of the text. Still, one can grant the point that cohesion is not logically necessary for coherence.

Is coherence a necessary consequence of cohesion? On this question Brown and Yule (1983:197) also give a negative answer, citing an example similar to (8) in chapter 5. In (8), successive sentences were composed by different people who knew that they were participating in an exercise to create text, but who had access only to the immediately preceding utterance. Thus, we find cohesive ties between contiguous sentences (rather remarkably, the idea of an upcoming meal is preserved throughout), yet (8) is not coherent, except perhaps with great imaginative effort and in bizarre ways. Strictly speaking, then, cohesion is neither necessary nor sufficient for coherence.

Yet cohesion is pervasive in discourse, and this suggests that it carries a heavy communicative load. Its importance to coherence is the importance of what we say to what we mean. That is, cohesion represents "hard data" to guide the hearer toward an adequate mental representation. Since cohesion is valuable for the hearer, knowledge of how to furnish the right kinds of cohesion is also valuable for the speaker.

Cohesion is likewise important to the text analyst. When you analyze discourse, especially without a native speaker's intuitions of language and culture, on what do you base your judgment of the text's coherence? On what basis can you construct a mental representation for it, whether internal or external? While cohesion does not provide the only answer (native speakers and the study of culture should help), it can certainly provide important evidence.

If text structure were merely linear, with sentences strung together like the cars in a train, each one merely being connected to the adjacent ones, there would be no way to account for the fact that example (8) is not a good text. The fact that it is not, indicates that text structure has an indispensable

hierarchical dimension (Tomlin et al. 1997:90). It is to this that we turn in
the following chapter.

Key Concepts:
cohesion
descriptive expressions alluding to earlier entities
identity
    repetition
    lexical replacement
    pronouns
    other pro-forms
    substitution
    ellipsis
lexical relations
    hyponymy
    part-whole
    collocation
morphosyntactic patterns
    consistency of inflectional categories
    echoic utterances
    discourse-pragmatic structuring
signals of relations between propositions
intonation patterns

7

Thematic Groupings and Thematic Discontinuities

7.1 Thematic groupings

Thus far, we have discussed very little in discourse that could be called structure. We have discussed:

- types of text (chapters 1–4);
- mental representations as the basis of coherence (chapter 5); and
- cohesive ties as linguistic signals of coherence (chapter 6).

However, with the possible exception of conversational turns (section 1.3), no discourse structure per se has yet been mentioned.

While we should not imagine structure where it does not exist, in most texts there are indeed signs of underlying structure. Even without looking at purely linguistic clues, we note that "within most [oral] narratives one finds certain places where the speaker pauses longer than normally, where there is likely to be an increase in fumbling and disfluency, and where an interlocutor is especially likely to contribute some encouraging noise or remark" (Chafe 1987:42f). In written narrative we commonly find other kinds of boundary phenomena, such as paragraph indentation and chapters. In plays, we find scenes and acts.

By such means the speaker, consciously or not, is grouping sentences into units of text, which we refer to as THEMATIC GROUPINGS. Paragraphing and similar signals constitute prima facie evidence that some kind of grouping is there.[19] More than that, groupings of different "sizes", e.g., chapters made up of paragraphs, acts made up of scenes, suggest that in longer or more complex texts, thematic groupings can be nested within each other in a hierarchical arrangement.

Why should this be? Why cannot texts just come as uniform strings of sentences? An answer is suggested by general principles of cognition. Humans typically process large amounts of information in CHUNKS, somewhat like we eat a meal in bites. This helps us deal with complexity: "a chunk functions as a unit in memory, so that we can remember about the same number of chunks regardless of how many lower-order units are used in their construction" (Paivio and Begg 1981:176). In a longer discourse there will indeed be many items of information; the speaker chunks material into parts which can be dealt with separately. What thematic groupings of sentences reflect, then, is conceptual chunking.[20]

7.2 Why chunk here?

If chunking in texts were no more than this, it would not matter where the chunks were made, as long as the pieces were "bite-size". However, it turns out that chunking is responsive to content as well as to size. "When one looks at the content of the narrative in such places [where pause, disfluency, etc., occur in spoken narrative], one usually discovers a significant change in scene, time, character configuration, event structure, and the like" (Chafe 1987:43).

This can be explained if we think of a mental representation (e.g., for a narrative) as being organized into sections, each of which is associated with particular places, times, participants, events, and perhaps other categories as well. That is, even though the mental representation for a coherent text is (by definition) a connected structure overall, its component parts have even tighter internal connections. If we could somehow get inside a mental representation and look around, we would find certain discontinuities between major sections.

---

[19]Not all types of written paragraphs reflect groupings that are motivated on conceptual grounds. Some are purely conventional, as paragraphing at changes of speaker. A single device (indentation) is used for multiple purposes. This is common with other typographical devices (periods, quotation marks, etc.).

[20]The distinction between conceptual organization and linguistic organization, encountered in chapter 6 in the coherence-cohesion dichotomy, is common in text analysis. See Pike and Pike's (1982) distinction between referential and grammatical organization, Longacre's (1996) distinction between notional and surface structure, and Grimes' (1975) distinction between content organization and cohesion relationships.

Chunking, then, is necessary so that people can handle large amounts of information, but discontinuities in content provide well-motivated occasions for it. We now look more closely at continuity and discontinuity in narrative.

7.3 Dimensions of thematic continuity in narrative

Givón (1984:245) speaks of THEMATIC CONTINUITY as holding within (part of) a text, and THEMATIC DISCONTINUITY for the "significant changes" noted by Chafe. Table (28) presents four commonly recognized thematic dimensions in narrative (time, place, action, participants).

(28) Dimensions of thematic continuity/discontinuity in narrative
      (based on Givón 1984:245)

Dimension	Continuity	Discontinuity
time	events separated by at most only small forward gaps	large forward gaps or events out of order
place	same place or (for motion) continuous change	discrete changes of place
action	all material of the same type: event, nonevent, conversation, etc.	change from one type of material to another
participants	same cast and same general roles vis-à-vis one other	discrete changes of cast or change in relative roles

In narrative, then, the speaker typically begins a new thematic grouping when there is a significant discontinuity in at least one of these four dimensions, and usually in more than one.[21] Within a thematic grouping, there is usually continuity along all four dimensions. One can think of a new thematic grouping resulting when the speaker leaves one section of the mental representation and moves on to, or perhaps creates, another.

---

[21]The presence of a single discontinuity does not necessarily imply a new thematic grouping. For example, double-difference contrasts (see chapter 11) typically involve a change of topic but often belong to the same thematic grouping, sometimes even to the same sentence. A thematic grouping, as the name implies, can generally be expected to consist of more than one sentence.

7.4 Cohesive ties and thematic groupings

In discourse of all kinds, it is common to find cohesive ties occurring in patterns that are based on thematic groupings. When this happens, it provides linguistic corroboration for groupings that the analyst might initially posit on conceptual grounds. We now look in turn at each one of Givón's four thematic dimensions and note typical patterns of cohesive ties.

TIME is especially important in narrative (section 2.1). Narrative events are typically in sequence, so there are continual small changes in time from one event to the next, even within a thematic grouping. Significant time gaps, however, generally result in new groupings. In fact, groupings in narrative are generally correlated more closely with time than with any other thematic dimension. As a result, expressions of time are commonly associated with the beginning of narrative groupings, especially when they are sentence-initial, as in (29).

(29) **So after waiting another two hours,** it was finally announced, "Train...will be leaving..."

(appendix B, line 19)

Another kind of temporal discontinuity is a FLASHBACK, since it is "set in a time earlier than the main action" *(Oxford English Dictionary)*. In English, flashbacks commonly have the pluperfect *(had...-ed),* as in (30).

(30) Belly-crawling clear of the garage before it disintegrated, Jim **had hooked** his muscular arms around the base of a pine tree.

(appendix A, line 29)

PLACE can also be important in narrative, with or without a change of time. In (31), there is a preposed expression of place.

(31) **About halfway there,** there was some nice couple...

(appendix B, line 59)

Expressions of either time or place can indicate new thematic groupings, especially when they are preposed, as in (29) and (31). The reason for this is that, cross-linguistically, preposed expressions often constitute special cohesive ties linking the following predication to something in the preceding context. This only needs to happen when the link has to be changed or updated in some way. Hence, preposed expressions often signal the onset of new thematic units; in narrative, preposed adverbial expressions most commonly play that role. Conversely, when adverbial expressions are present but not preposed, no significant discontinuity is being signaled, and no new thematic grouping is being signaled either (Levinsohn 2000:14). This is the case with (32).

(32)   So, we got on a lovely train **in Duluth.**

(appendix B, line 4)

Preposed adverbial (and other) expressions will be discussed in section 11.4.1.

One common change of ACTION that is marked cross-linguistically is when a story moves from reported conversation to nonspeech events. Changes in action are often marked by the use of a sentence-initial conjunction such as "so" or "then". In the story found in appendix B, for instance, *so* occurs when the action changes from reported conversation to nonspeech events in lines 14 and 19 as in (29). Shifts from thought to action may be similarly marked.

(33)   And we thought that...it might be safer and wiser if we took the train...
So, we got on a lovely train in Duluth.

(appendix B, lines 2,4)

Another common change of action is between events and nonevents, as illustrated in appendix A, line 8.

(34)   Jim, who'd been stowing away patio furniture, liked to call his slightly built wife Toughie, because of her energy and determination.

PARTICIPANTS are obviously important in discourse, and patterns of participant reference will be dealt with in chapters 16–18. Here, we simply note that the introduction of a participant (with a full noun phrase) is sometimes the occasion of a new thematic grouping, as in the story of the Three Little Pigs.

(35)   The first little pig...
The second litle pig...
The third little pig...

Participants are usefully distinguished from props. PROPS (e.g., the train in (32)) have only a passive role in the story; they never *do* anything significant (Grimes 1975:43ff). Participants, on the other hand, take an active role. For this reason, participants are usually either persons or personifications, e.g., animals given human qualities. Note, however, that not all persons in a narrative are participants. Participants and props often use different patterns of reference, some of which pattern with respect to thematic groupings; see chapters 16–18.

Having surveyed the four major dimensions of thematic continuity, we now summarize linguistic signals typical of thematic boundaries as shown in (36).

(36)   Linguistic signals typical of thematic boundaries

Initial in a grouping, it is common to find:
- a preposed expression, especially one of time, place, or topic
- particles ("Well," "Now"), or the absence of the normal particle
- sentence connectors ("Then," "So") or the absence of the normal connector
- participants referred to by full noun phrases instead of pronouns, etc.

Initial or final in a grouping, it is common to find:
- changes in the tense/aspect of verbs
- summary ("That's what they did") or evaluation ("So that was exciting")

Between groupings in an oral text, it is common to find:
- pause, hesitation, or break in timing
- change in pitch of intonation contour

As has been mentioned, thematic dimensions can be updated at a thematic boundary even when they do not manifest a discontinuity. There seem to be two reasons for this. First, a given genre may associate thematic breaks with updating in one particular dimension; this is the case for time in narrative, as we noted earlier. Second, speakers frequently use the onset of a thematic grouping to do a general update. In narrative, for example, participants are often referred to by full noun phrases even when they are not new to the scene and there is little danger of ambiguity.

Since thematic boundaries are points of reorientation, general updating should not be surprising.

The following should also be noted:

> Change of orientation is not something which is simply present or absent at certain points in the narrative. It is present or absent to varying degrees at different points. Two reasons suggest themselves for why change in orientation may be a matter of degree. First, we have identified various components of an orientation, not just one, and one or two or all of these components may be present at any particular point of transition. Changes of space, time, people, etc., tend to cluster, but they need not all be present at the same point. Beyond that, the components themselves are scalar: there may be more or less of a change in protagonists, more or less of a shift in background activity. (Chafe 1980:45)

Points of major reorientation are the easiest to recognize; points of minor reorientation are more questionable. Often, minor groupings occur within major ones.[22]

7.5 Practical considerations

Signals of thematic groupings are generally indirect: few if any elements have the gloss 'thematic boundary'. Rather, boundary signals work because they pattern in characteristic ways with respect to boundaries. However, if we need boundaries to recognize patterns and patterns to recognize boundaries, there is more than a little danger of circularity.

To the extent that this dilemma can be resolved, the solution will be found in the convergence of a large amount of evidence of diverse types. Intuitive judgments of conceptual chunks and cross-linguistically common patterns of elements, when taken together, constitute independent evidence for boundaries. When they converge with a high degree of consistency, the hypotheses merit confidence.

The following, then, is a rough procedure that can be useful in the beginning stages of segmenting a text into thematic groupings:

---

[22]"Discourse is neither flat nor linear in its organization; it is hierarchical," with "three levels of organization and development: clause level or local; paragraph or episode; and overall text or discourse or global." However, "the embedding of lower level units into higher ones is ultimately recursive" (Tomlin et al. 1997:66, 90).

(37) Practical steps in segmenting texts into thematic groupings

    a. On the basis of your mental representation of the text, and using your linguistic instincts from whatever source, make initial guesses as to where thematic discontinuities might be.

    b. In those places, look for linguistic signals that pattern with respect to the intuitive groupings, especially those which have been found to signal such boundaries cross-linguistically.

    c. Where linguistic signals and instinctive groupings fail to match, revise your groupings or your hypotheses or both, guided by plausibility, in order to come up with better hypotheses.

    d. Test and revise your hypotheses with other text data.

Key Concepts:
thematic groupings
conceptual chunking
thematic continuity and discontinuity
four dimensions of thematic continuity in narrative
    time
       flashback
    place
    action
    participants (versus props)
preposed adverbial expressions

8

Text Charting

You can observe a lot just by watching. Yogi Berra

TEXT CHARTING refers to the visual display of a text in such a way as to make features of interest apparent (by lining them up, for instance). This definition suggests why text charting is useful: texts are very complex phenomena, with different dimensions of organization. A well-designed chart can bring out specific dimensions of interest, and thus serve as a heuristic tool for analysis and understanding.

The definition also suggests that there can be more than one way to go about text charting, depending on what features of text organization you are interested in at a particular point. You can design different kinds of charts with particular features in view; they will, of course, reflect your own assumptions as to how texts are organized with respect to these features. As you work with text charting, feel free to think about ways you might want to design charts, or modify existing designs, to "get at" text features you are interested in.

In this chapter we present one way to chart a text, together with a particular application of it to thematic groupings. This charting reflects a general-purpose design for early stages of text analysis, and is based on extensive field analysis of discourse (Longacre and Levinsohn 1978).[23]

---

[23]Different practitioners of discourse analysis have preferred ways of charting; see, for example, Grimes 1975, chapter 6 for the "Thurman chart".

8.1 What kind of text should I begin with?

For beginning text analysis, narrative usually yields the best results and is best understood. The text should have a moderate amount of complexity, since the point of the exercise is to see how complexity is handled. Specifically, it should have two or more major participants,[24] as well as a problem, conflict, or area of tension, along with its resolution.

According to Grimes (1975:33), "the texts that yield the most consistent analysis are edited texts." These will approximate what might be thought of as the text analyst's version of competence (accepted uses of the resources of the language), as contrasted with performance (including incidental mistakes, infelicitous choices, etc.). Although editing generally implies that the text is in written form, it could be one that was originally recorded, then transcribed. The editing should be done by a member of the language community (by the original author of the text, if possible) to preserve the author's mental representation and stylistic preferences (section 3.1).[25]

Ideally, the text should be by a person who has "a reputation for consistently producing the kind of discourse that other people want to listen to" (loc. cit.). This will also help insure that the text is well formed.

Before charting the text, you need to "control the facts of the discourse", i.e., "know who did what to whom, and, as far as possible, what relation one action has to the other actions in its immediate context" (Longacre and Levinsohn 1978:111). This means that you should have a fairly complete picture of the text world and of the external contextualization as well. For this, you should get a free translation of the story and then ask specific questions. As a side benefit of this process, you will gain cultural insights.

8.2 The basic chart

The kind of chart proposed here displays similar grammatical constituents in the same column; sentences are set off from one another by horizontal lines. This presupposes a text already segmented into sentences, with sentences parsed into their constituents; alternatively, you can do that in the process of charting.

Turn an A4 or 8½ x 11 inch sheet *sideways,* then divide into four main columns, as follows:[26]

---

[24]See section 17.2.1 for discussion of major participants.

[25]Of course, a version with errors and disfluencies would have its own value for the analyst. It might show cognitive processes more transparently, but good discourse form less transparently.

[26]The columns reflect what has been posited as a universal set of positions for sentence elements (Dik 1978, Van Valin 1993:10). See chapter 11 for further discussion.

Column 1: introducers and left-dislocated elements [27]
Column 2: elements which are preposed but are still tightly con-
          nected to the main predication
Column 3: the nuclear predication itself, with three to five
          subcolumns (see below)
Column 4: adjunct and right-dislocated elements which follow the
          nuclear predication

Divide column 3 into three to five subcolumns and select appropriate
subcolumns for the nuclear subject and verb so that the most neutral order of constituents within the clause is reflected. For instance, if the most
neutral order of constituents is S-V-IO-O, no constituent separates the subject from the verb, and it is unusual for more than three constituents to
follow the verb, then allocate four subcolumns as follows (column 4 may
be used for the third post-verbal constituent):

S—V—(IO)—(O)

The IO and O subcolumns may be used for other constituents when necessary (e.g., predicate complements, post-verbal subjects). Any nuclear constituents that are preposed are allocated to column 2. The page might then be
divided as follows:

	column 1	column 2	column 3				column 4
reference	introducers and left-dislocated	preposed elements	S	V	(IO)	(O)	post-nuclear elements

Similarly, if the most neutral order of constituents is S-IO-O-V and it is
unusual for more than three constituents to occur between the subject and
the verb, then allocate five subcolumns as follows:

	column 1	column 2	column 3				column 4
reference	introducers and left-dislocated	preposed elements	S	(IO)	(O)	V	post-nuclear elements

---

[27]See section 11.4 for discussion of left- and right-dislocated elements.

NOTE:

- The relative width, order, and number of columns and subcolumns depends on the individual language and often also on the text genre. In practice, the first page or two of the first text in each genre may need to be charted several times to find the optimal way of allocating columns.
- Do NOT be tempted to use very wide paper and multiply columns! The eye is unable to take in at a glance a text spread over the width of an accounts book.
- Finite clauses that are dependent may be charted either as though they were nuclear predications (i.e., in column 3) or in the appropriate column for pre-nuclear or post-nuclear elements.

8.3 Conventions for charting

As you write the text on the chart you have prepared, follow these conventions:

1. Start a new line for every new clause.
2. Put a line across the page before every new sentence.
3. If a consultant is likely to be helping you with text analysis, include a word-by-word (and where relevant, morpheme-by-morpheme) translation into the consultant's language.
4. Do not rearrange the order of constituents.
   - If a constituent is in an "unusual" position, put "post-verb", "pre-verb", etc., in the appropriate column, but record the constituent according to its actual place of occurrence.
   - Move down the page, when it is not possible to move to the right and employ the correct column (e.g., if three constituents occur between the subject and verb, but only two columns are available).
5. Mark implicit constituents (especially subjects, and objects of transitive verbs) by a dash: ——.
6. Use underlining or a different color for reported speech.
7. Number the sentences/text units in a narrow initial column (headed "reference").

As an alternative to charting by hand, you may wish to enhance an interlinear display produced by a computer program. You should follow the numbered conventions above as far as you are able! In particular:

1. Start a new line for each new **clause,** but preserve sentence level numbering, if possible.
2. Use different **styles** to distinguish:
   - new lines representing a new clause versus a new sentence, e.g., by extra space before each new sentence,
   - language material from glosses, and
   - reported speech.
3. Use **tabs** to line up corresponding material (e.g., the presence versus absence of coordinating conjunctions, subjects, verbs).

8.4 Indicating thematic groupings

The first kind of analysis recommended here is to identify thematic groupings in the text. This is perhaps the most important analytical step, since many other organizational features of text build upon it. The basic chart described above is designed to enable you to begin to analyze thematic groupings.

At some point, indicate your initial guess as to thematic groupings, as described in step 1 of (37) in section 7.5. Group together those sentences that seem to naturally belong together, and divide the discourse at those points at which it seems to naturally separate (Longacre and Levinsohn 1978:118).

The following table displays a possible first step in an intuitive analysis into thematic groupings of lines 1–9 of the text in appendix A. The sentence numbers are listed vertically. Boxes enclose those sentences that seem to naturally belong together, with boxes inside boxes to denote groupings of groupings. Horizontal lines indicate the points at which there seem to be divisions in the discourse. Words to the left and right of the table respectively indicate possible linguistic signals and observations about the analysis.

(38)

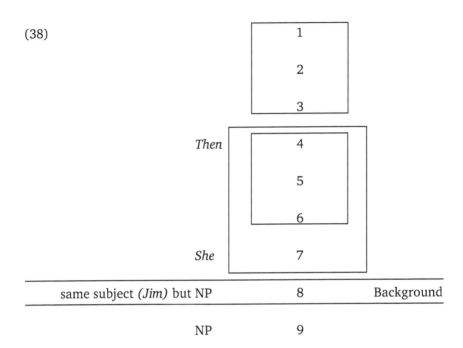

You are now ready to revise your groupings on the basis of patterns of cohesive links, following steps 2–4 of (37). Take note of the patterning of elements referred to in (36) of section 7.4, which could provide evidence for thematic groupings.

> **Key Concept:**
> text charting

9

Mental Representations Revisited

Ninety-nine percent of this game is half mental. Yogi Berra

Thus far, mental representations have been invoked for an understanding of coherence (chapter 5) and thematic groupings (chapter 7). They have much more to offer. In these next chapters, they will help us understand the following aspects of discourse organization (presented in roughly increasing linguistic levels):

- words and phrases: activation status and referential status (chapter 10);
- sentence: discourse-pragmatic structuring (chapter 11);
- sentence and higher: kinds of information, foregrounding and backgrounding (chapter 12);
- sentence and higher: semantic relations (chapter 13);
- sentence and higher: reported conversation (chapter 14); and
- major sections: conventionalized organization (chapter 15).

For these topics, we will need a sharper notion of mental representations. Here we have a problem: no one knows for sure what the structure of mental representations is in the brain. The best we can do is to construct a mental representation of mental representations, based on how they seem to behave in psychological tests and language. The present chapter, then, provides us with a framework for further understanding of discourse.

9.1 What mental representations represent

As you probably suspect by now, mental representations are not limited to understanding discourse, but are basic tools of human cognition. They "play a central and unifying role in representing objects, states of affairs, sequences of events, the way the world is, and the social and psychological actions of daily life"; in general, a mental representation can be thought of as representing a "state of affairs" (Johnson-Laird 1983:397f).[28] Discourse is simply a way "to create representations comparable to those deriving from direct acquaintance with the world" (loc. cit.).

9.2 Hierarchy

In the following discussion we will use the term SCHEMA to refer to a network or "cluster of interrelated expectations" (Chafe 1987:29) which is available from the culture.[29] Probably the most important structural feature of schemata (the plural of schema) is their HIERARCHICAL ARRANGEMENT. In the following description, most of what Adams and Collins say about schemata applies to other kinds of mental representations as well.

> A schema is a description of a particular class of concepts and is composed of a hierarchy of schemata embedded within schemata. The representation at the top of the hierarchy is sufficiently general to capture the essential aspects of all members of the class. For example, if the conceptual class represented by the schema were "going to a restaurant" (Schank and Abelson 1977), its top level would include such information as that a restaurant is a commercial establishment where people pay money to have someone else prepare their food and clean up after them. At the level beneath this global characterization are more specific schemata (e.g., going to a diner, going to a fast hamburger operation, going to a swanky restaurant). In general, as one moves down the hierarchy, the number of embedded schemata multiplies while the scope of each narrows, until, at the lowest level, the schemata apply to unique perceptual events. (1979:3)

---

[28]Mental representations need to handle both events and states, but it is not yet clear what kind of a general structure does both. The term "state of affairs" is intended to cover both categories.

[29]Other terms which have been used, often confusingly, for this and related notions, are *script, frame, scenario* (see Tannen 1979; Brown and Yule 1983:236ff).

The type of hierarchy discussed by Adams and Collins is **taxonomic,** involving different kinds of restaurants. Mental hierarchies can also involve different **parts of a whole.** In a restaurant representation, whole-part subdivisions might include "entering and being seated", "ordering", "eating the meal", and "paying and exiting". In either kind of hierarchy, a narrative discourse involving a restaurant presents "unique perceptual events", some of which might not actually be part of a typical restaurant schema. The hearer has the task of finding or constructing an appropriate representation into which the facts of the discourse will fit (1979:3).

9.3 Concepts

Mental representations can be thought of as composed of elements that are entities, properties, or relations (Johnson-Laird 1983:398). ENTITIES correspond to what we prototypically refer to with nouns, and can perhaps be pictured as NODES in the representation (de Beaugrande and Dressler 1981:98ff). PROPERTIES are qualities that describe entities and can be thought of as tags attached to nodes. RELATIONS associate entities, and can be thought of as labeled lines connecting nodes, the labels indicating different roles in the relation. A special kind of relation would be an event or action. Entities, properties, and relations are sometimes referred to by the cover term CONCEPTS.

A concept in a mental representation can be thought of as embodying a SLOT, which "can accept any of the range of values that are compatible" (Adams and Collins 1979:4). For example, in a restaurant schema, one would likely have slots for waiters and a bar or counter; these would be unfilled slots unless and until they were instantiated. If it turns out that a particular restaurant situation turns out to have a counter, that slot would be filled; if it is established that there is no counter, that slot would presumably be deleted from the mental representation. "The comprehension of a specific situation or story involves the process of instantiation whereby elements in the situation are bound to appropriate slots" (loc. cit.). If it is not known whether the particular restaurant has a counter, that slot might remain in the mental representation, but without being filled. Certain slots are virtually certain of being filled (food, for example, in a restaurant); others may only be said to be plausible (e.g., a children's play area or live music).

9.4 Arriving at mental representations

As discourse hearers and perceivers of situations in general, we have two general strategies for arriving at mental representations: bottom-up processing and top-down processing (Adams and Collins 1979:5). BOTTOM-UP PROCESSING begins with "unique perceptual events" which will eventually occupy the lower levels of the hierarchy, and constructs successive generalizations to make sense of the data. For example, we may hear of people sitting at tables and asking other people for food to be brought to them; we may note that payment is involved, and that those who eat do not clean up, etc., and only after all the individual facts are in do we form a judgment of what is going on. This is an excruciatingly costly way to process information. When possible, we make use of TOP-DOWN PROCESSING, in which, confronted with a certain range of facts, we quite early "jump to a hypothesis" ("Oh, that must be a restaurant!"). This involves bringing in an entire schema, with all of its ready-made, "off-the-shelf" structure and unfilled slots, and checking to see how well it fits the facts we are being given. Even if it needs some adjusting, a schema that is brought in as a whole, on a trial basis, generally saves much effort.

Top-down processing, then, involves a whole structure of expectations to be checked out. Where do such EXPECTATION STRUCTURES come from? There are two principal sources: experience (either personal or collective, which we call culture) and the discourse itself (Brown and Yule 1983:235). Experience and culture give rise to the restaurant schema mentioned above. The second source of expectation structures is the text itself (or, more generally, the situation being perceived). Take a narrative, for example. Often, when presented with raw data (e.g., boy meets girl), the hearer (operating in a top-down mode) makes a PROJECTION FROM THE DATA as to what might happen. Some projections are more speculative and tentative (will boy marry girl?), while others involve smaller steps with stronger expectations (boy will grow interested in girl, meet her again, etc.). Certain types of discourse organization seem designed to generate such projections (e.g., repetition: what happened when the first little pig built a house, what happened when the second little pig built a house, etc.). It then becomes a point of interest with the hearer to see whether his or her projections are fulfilled.

Many expectation structures have their source both in the culture and in the text. Whatever their source, though, they are powerful devices which aid the hearer in arriving at a mental representation and maintaining interest in the text.

Optimally, "top-down and bottom-up processing should be occurring...simultaneously. The data that are needed to instantiate or fill out the schemata become available through bottom-up processing; top-down processing facilitates their assimilation", once a promising expectation structure is invoked (Adams and Collins 1979:5).

Key Concepts:

schema

hierarchical arrangement

    nodes

concepts

    entities

    properties

    relations/events

strategies for arriving at mental representations

    bottom-up processing

    top-down processing

        expectation structures

        projection from the data

10

Activation Status, Definiteness, and Referential Status

In chapter 9 we suggested that experience and culture lead humans unconsciously to construct schemata which they then access in appropriate situations. This means "that our minds contain very large amounts of knowledge or information" (Chafe 1987:22). Nevertheless, it seems reasonable to assume "that only a very small amount of this information can be focused on, or be 'active', at any one time" (loc. cit.).

> Chafe...argues that a particular "concept"[as defined in section 9.3[30]] may be in any one of three ACTIVATION STATES, which he calls ACTIVE,...ACCESSIBLE and INACTIVE, respectively. An ACTIVE concept is one "that is currently lit up, a concept in a person's consciousness at a particular moment." An ACCESSIBLE...concept is "one that is in a person's peripheral consciousness, a concept of which a person has a background awareness, but one that is not being directly focused on." An INACTIVE concept is one "that is currently in a person's long-term memory, neither focally nor peripherally active." (Lambrecht 1994:93f)[31]

Because active concepts are "currently lit up", they are sometimes referred to as "given information". Inactive concepts, in turn, become "new information" at the time that they are activated. As an illustration, consider the

---

[30]Lambrecht himself refers to concepts as "(mental representations of) referents" (1994:94).

[31]For further reading on this topic, see Chafe 1987 and Lambrecht 1994:93–100.

utterance, *I saw Mary yesterday. She says hello.* If there has been no previous reference to Mary in the current conversation, then she was an inactive concept in the hearer's mind until the first sentence was uttered (the speaker assumes that the hearer has this Mary in his or her long-term memory). Once reference has been made to her, however, she becomes an active concept.

Accessible concepts are of three kinds.

- Firstly, a concept may be accessible "through deactivation from an earlier state, typically by having been active at an earlier point in the discourse." In line 50 of appendix B, for instance, *Omaha* is an accessible concept because it had been an active one earlier in the discourse (it was last mentioned in line 27).

- Secondly, a concept may be accessible because it "belongs to the set of expectations associated with a schema" (Chafe 1987:29). In line 27 of appendix B, *the train station* is an accessible concept; even though it has not previously been mentioned, because the discourse concerns trains and one gets on trains in stations.

- Finally, there are concepts "whose accessible status is due to their presence in the text-external world" (Lambrecht 1994:99). Such is the case with *the northwest* in appendix A, line 2.

Activation status is one example of what we might call the COGNITIVE STATUS of concepts. In this chapter we consider cognitive statuses of different types. Beginning with Chafe's three-way classification of activation status, we will pass on to consider definiteness (including generic references) and referential status.

10.1 Activation status: three processes

For each of the three activation states considered above (active, accessible, inactive), Chafe discusses how a concept acquires that status and how the status is typically manifested. Three processes are involved: activation (including reactivation), deactivation, and maintenance in an active state.[32]

In ACTIVATION, a concept goes from inactive or accessible to active status.

- The activation of a concept from *inactive status,* resulting in "new information", "evidently exacts a greater cost in terms of cognitive effort than any other kind" (Chafe 1987:31). It is only accomplished by expending weighty coding resources (e.g., heavy stress).

---

[32]In the following paragraphs, some of Chafe's material is slightly recast from the point of view of these processes.

- The activation of a concept that was previously only *accessible* generally does not require heavy coding. It does, however, require a mention of the concept and, if the language has the means to do so, it requires a signal of its former accessible status, such as the definite article in English.

DEACTIVATION "probably exacts no cost at all", since a concept is being allowed simply to revert from the active to the accessible state.

MAINTENANCE refers to keeping a concept in an active status, and is an in-between process as regards coding resources.[33] Maintaining a concept in active status requires a minimum of coding resources, provided there is no ambiguity. Hence, "given concepts are spoken with an attenuated pronunciation", are often pronominalized, and sometimes undergo ellipsis (Chafe 1987:26).

From these processes, then, we see that the amount of coding material required varies directly with the cognitive effort required. In particular, heavier coding is used where the cognitive status undergoes more change. We return to this principle in section 16.2.

We close this section by mentioning Chafe's ONE NEW CONCEPT AT A TIME CONSTRAINT. In informal oral narrative, "only one concept can be changed from the inactive to the active state during any one initial pause" (Chafe 1987:31f). The activation of a concept that was previously *accessible* is not bound by this constraint, however. Furthermore, there are common types of written material where the constraint does not hold, since in such writing "it is hard to find anything like idea [intonation] units" (Chafe 1985b:107).

The following extract is from an oral text about a college class that Chafe (1987:32) uses to illustrate the "one new concept at a time constraint." Given concepts are placed in the first column, accessible concepts in the second, and new concepts in the third. The sentence numbers are Chafe's.

(39)

	Given concepts	Accessible concepts	New concepts
4.		*éverybody* *the instructor*	lóved
5.	*(he)*		**was a real óld**
	guy		**world Swiss**
6.	*(this)*		**was a biólogy**
	course		

---

[33]Nothing need be said about maintaining a concept in inactive status.

10.2 Definiteness

Whereas Chafe supplies a three-way opposition for activation status, there is a closely related two-way opposition that some languages encode: definite versus indefinite reference. A DEFINITE REFERENT is one which the speaker assumes that the hearer will be able to identify, i.e., to locate in his or her current mental representation. An INDEFINITE REFERENT is one for which the speaker is instructing the hearer to create a slot (Chafe 1976:55). This is the difference between *the garage door* (appendix A, line 7) and *a piece of lumber* (line 19), as indicated by the articles.

Even in languages which commonly signal this distinction, some expressions are indeterminate *(I saw **this big buck**)*. In such cases, the (in)definiteness of the concept must be judged on the basis of contextual clues.

Some languages use constituent order instead of articles to signal the definite-indefinite distinction. In Ojibwa, an Algonquian language, Tomlin and Rhodes (1979) argue that definite nouns typically follow the verb, while indefinites precede the verb. (It is usually claimed that most languages show the opposite pattern.)

Some languages do not signal the definite-indefinite distinction except under special discourse conditions. In Mbyá Guaraní, where there are no articles, indefiniteness is signaled only when introducing an important entity. Under such circumstances, the number one precedes the noun (see further in section 17.2.1).

10.3 Generic reference

In a generic reference, the speaker has in mind a particular *class* of entities: ***Deer** are beautiful animals*. Since the speaker also expects the hearer to be able to identify the class, generic reference has much in common with definiteness. In fact, the two are often coded the same *(**The deer** is a beautiful animal)* and have similar syntax (in many languages, topics in a topic-comment structure must be either definite or generic). On the other hand, some languages treat generics as a subclass of indefinites.

10.4 Referential status

Mental representations play an important role not only in definiteness, but also in regard to referential status. However, whereas definiteness has to do with whether the *hearer* can be expected to identify the referent, referential status has to do with whether the *speaker* is attempting to make a specific reference. That is, a REFERENTIAL entity is one for which the speaker is using an instantiated slot in his or her mental representation; a NONREFERENTIAL or nonspecific entity is one for which the speaker is not using such a slot. Thus, a speaker who says *I saw a/the/this big buck* is being referential (on any of these three possibilities), since he or she has a specific buck in mind. However, if the speaker says *I went deer hunting,* there is nothing to indicate that he or she has a specific deer in mind.

As with definiteness, there are also indeterminate forms in referentiality: the noun phrase *a deer* in *I'm going to look for a deer* could be intended either referentially or nonreferentially, depending on whether the speaker had a specific deer in mind. It is common to find nonreferential expressions incorporated with the verb (e.g., *deer hunting*).

Furthermore, there are languages that do not attempt to make a formal distinction for referentiality except under special circumstances. From the definitions given, it follows that definite entities are always referential: if the speaker expects the hearer to be able to identify a specific entity, then the speaker would also need to have that specific entity in mind.

10.5 More on activation status

The three activation states discussed by Chafe (active, accessible, inactive) are linguistically attested in all languages. However, we must recognize that boundaries between states are likely to be fuzzy. Perceptually, there are bound to be many degrees of activation of entities; simply note that entities gradually fade from consciousness after being activated, unless their active status is maintained. Yet, in talking about them, speakers must choose from a range of discrete coding devices (e.g., pronouns). So the activation status of a concept is, in the final analysis, what the speaker chooses to present it to be, rather than what the analyst feels that it should be.

Key Concepts:
activation states
    active concepts ("given information")
    accessible concepts
    inactive concepts ("new information")
cognitive status
processes relating to activation states
    activation
    deactivation
    maintenance in active status
"one new concept at a time" constraint
definiteness
    definite
    indefinite
generic reference
referential status
    referential
    nonreferential

11

Discourse-Pragmatic Structuring of Sentences

He said, "I am not a thief," with so slight an emphasis on the first word that it was just possible he was not impertinent. (Graham Greene, *The heart of the matter*)

Sentences that have the same semantic (propositional) content can be expressed in different ways.

(40) Joe milked the goat.
      The goat, Joe milked.
      It was the goat that Joe milked.
      It was Joe who milked the goat.
      Joe's the one who milked the goat.
      The one who milked the goat was Joe.
      What Joe did to the goat was milk it.
      What Joe did was milk the goat.
      What got milked by Joe was the goat.

All this occurs in language, even without considering the nuances of intonation that are rarely noted in written material. Why should there be such a variety of ways to say essentially the same thing? The reason is that the speaker can relate the pieces of information in a proposition in different ways to what the hearer is already aware of, i.e., to his or her current mental representation. This results in different forms of DISCOURSE-PRAGMATIC STRUCTURING which is a type of cohesion, as noted in 6.4. In all communication, the

61

speaker guides the hearer in adding material to his or her mental representation; semantic content relates to *what* is added, whereas discourse-pragmatic structuring relates to *where* it is added and *how* it relates to what is already there.

In particular, some pieces of information merely point to something already present in the hearer's mental representation, while other pieces are intended to change what is there. With that difference we begin.

11.1 Focus and scope of focus

For a given utterance, it is extremely helpful for the hearer to know what is the most important or salient change to be made in his or her mental representation. The part of the utterance that specifies this, we define as its FOCUS. In other words, the focus of an utterance is that part which indicates what the speaker intends as the most important or salient change to be made in the hearer's mental representation.[34]

Material in focus typically (1) adds new information or (2) changes what is already present in an activated propositional framework, either by replacement or by selecting between alternatives. This means that focused material is generally (1) new or (2) contrastive (Dik et al. 1981).[35] (New material can also be added in an activated propositional framework, but need not be; contrast is discussed later in this chapter.) Every utterance has a focus.

(41)   Your **daughter** just killed a BEAR.

In (41), the CAPS indicate that we are considering a pronunciation with the intonation nucleus (primary sentence stress) on *bear;* the bolding indicates secondary stress on *daughter.*

The SCOPE OF FOCUS for a given sentence can vary with the context. To reflect this, Lambrecht proposes three types of focus structure. In answer to a question like "What happened?", the entire sentence (41) would be in focus (SENTENCE FOCUS). In answer to a question like "What's going on with my daughter?", the predicate *just killed a bear* would be the focus (PREDICATE FOCUS). Finally, in answer to a question such as "What did my daughter just kill?", *a bear* would be the focus (ARGUMENT FOCUS). Such formal ambiguity

---

[34]This definition is based on, but differs from, definitions of focus given by Lambrecht (1994:213: information "whereby the assertion differs from the presupposition") and Dik et al. (1981:42: "what is relatively the most important or salient information in the given setting").

[35]In addition, it is possible to refocus on given information, such as when the speaker is not certain that the hearer understood correctly.

due to scope of focus is generally clarified by the context (Chomsky 1971:199ff; Sperber and Wilson 1986:202ff).

While Lambrecht's types of scope for focus serve well as answers to the above questions in English, variations of constituent order *within a predicate focus* are often found in text material. Consequently, we find it useful to identify a smaller constituent as focus. For this reason, we will use the term COMMENT as an alternative for "predicate focus", and speak of the smaller focused constituent as FOCUS PROPER or simply "focus"; see section 11.3.

11.2 Focus, topic, and sentence articulations

We now look at sentences with different types of articulation (Andrews 1985:77ff).

In sentences with TOPIC-COMMENT articulation, topic is the entity that the utterance is primarily about (Dik 1978:130), while part or all of the comment is the focus, depending on the context. When (41) has topic-comment articulation, for instance, *your daughter* is topic and *just killed a bear* is comment, comprising predicate focus. In most languages, the topic regularly precedes the comment in sentences with topic-comment articulation (Hixkaryana is an exception—Derbyshire 1985); new (inactive) topics apparently are not final in any language (Gundel 1988:229). The matter of topic is further discussed in section 11.4.1.

Focus and topic are examples of PRAGMATIC ROLES (Comrie 1989:62), so named in analogy to semantic roles such as agent and patient; they are also called pragmatic functions (Dik 1978:128) or pragmatic relations, in analogy with grammatical relations.

Sentences with PRESENTATIONAL articulation serve "to introduce an entity whose semantic role is normally expressed with the subject function" (Andrews 1985:80; see also Lambrecht 1994:39 and Givón 1990:742ff). The intonation nucleus is generally on that entity, as in (42), which introduces (activates) the entity 'bear'.

(42)   There's a BEAR in here!

Many, perhaps all, languages have presentational sentences in which such a noun phrase follows a verb of existence, appearance, or emergence.

However, other kinds of presentational sentences have no special syntax:

(43)   (Watch out!) That CHIMNEY's falling down!

Cruttenden (1986) calls (43) an *event sentence:* it describes an event but is also presentational, as if drawing attention to the subject *chimney* effectively draws attention to the event. In both (42) and (43), the (notional) subject has the intonation nucleus, but the entire sentence presents new information (Cruttenden 1986:83; Lambrecht 1994:143f).

In sentences with FOCUS-PRESUPPOSITION articulation (Chomsky 1971:199ff; Andrews 1985:79f; Givón 1990, chapter 16),[36] just one concept is being asserted and the rest of the information is presupposed; the focused material fills a slot in an already-activated propositional framework. Example (41) would have focus-presupposition articulation in answer to a question such as "What did my daughter just kill? "; the presupposition would be "Your daughter just killed X", where X is an unfilled slot in the mental representation.

Focus-presupposition sentences generally have argument focus, and often show special syntax, morphology, or intonation (sometimes called "marked focus" constructions, as in Crozier 1984).[37] If a language makes different constructions available for argument focus, they will differ somewhat in their conditions of use (Givón 1990:704). In many languages, an element with argument focus is simply fronted (and given the intonation nucleus). This sounds a bit odd in English, especially if the focused element is new, indefinite information.

(44)   Focus —Presupposition—
        ? A BEAR your daughter killed.

English can, however, accomplish the same pragmatic effect with a bit of special syntax.

(45)   —Focus—— ——Presupposition——
        It was a BEAR that your daughter killed.

(45) is a CLEFT sentence: it has two clauses, the first of which contains the focused concept. According to Gundel (1988:231), "every language has cleft constructions."

In English, argument focus is most often signaled by intonation alone.

(46)   ——Focus—— -Presupposition-
        Your DAUGHTER killed that bear.

---

[36]"Presupposed" here is used in a pragmatic sense, rather than a formal logical one; in declaratives, pragmatically presupposed information is that which the speaker assumes the hearer will accept without its being specifically asserted (Givón 1984:256).

[37]Sometimes this is called "narrow focus" as opposed to "broad focus" (Cruttenden 1986:81). The three-way distinction adopted here is more useful.

(46) is unambiguous as to focus because the intonation center is not in its default position, as it is in (2).

(47)   (I didn't say "*except*",)
       I said "*Accept*".

The focus domain ("argument") in (47) is a single syllable which is surrounded by the presupposition; (47) is also contrastive (see below).

In focus-presupposition structuring, the presupposition is typically spoken with little stress, due to its typically being given (activated) information. In fact, it is often shortened or deleted altogether:

(48)   (Who killed that bear?)

       a.   ——Focus—— Presupposition
            Your DAUGHTER did.

       b.   ——Focus—— Presupposition
            Your DAUGHTER ∅.

The focus, however, cannot undergo ellipsis, since the utterance then would be missing its communicational "point".

11.3 General signals of focus

English is like many other languages in that the intonation nucleus (primary sentence stress) always falls within the focused constituent (Gundel 1988:230). Only a few languages, mostly tonal, do not use intonation as a signal of focus.[38] Written English can sometimes use italics, bolding, or underlining for the same purpose. Written language, however, poses problems for discourse-pragmatic structuring in general: not only are spoken signals often unavailable or grossly underrepresented, but the information structure is generally more complex (Chafe 1985b:111f).

The unmarked position for the intonation nucleus in English is on the final lexical item of the utterance (Cruttenden 1986:82). Expressions are sometimes maneuvered to final position in order for the intonation nucleus to fall on them, thus being clearly indicated as the focus proper

---

[38]Certain tonal languages in West Africa (e.g., Aghem, in Watters 1979:138; Ifè, in Marquita Klaver, pers. com.) are reported not to use intonation to signal focus. At least one nontonal language, Hixkaryana of Brazil (Derbyshire 1985:146), does not signal focus in that way either.

(Bolinger 1952).[39] This seems to be the motivation for (49b) as opposed to (49a).

(49)   a. I gave a book to JOHN.
       b. I gave John a BOOK.

Some languages signal focus by means of special particles, as in the following sentence from Ifè, a Yoruboid language of Togo (Marquita Klaver, pers. com.):

(50)   ——Focus—
       òngu   **ní**   dzé ìfó-mi   é
       3SG.EMPH FOC be older.brother-1SG.POSS   DEF
       HE's the one who is my older brother.

In (50), the particle *ní* signals contrastive focus on the pronoun *òngu* 'he' (in contrast to someone else).

All languages, in fact, appear to have modifiers that collocate with, hence help to signal, argument focus (Jackendoff 1972:249; Givón 1990:715). This is the case with the English noun modifier *even*.

(51)   Even JOHN didn't care to eat it.

Most languages have special constructions with an item in argument focus followed by the remainder of the clause, which provides the associated presupposition. The cleft construction of (45) is one example. When this means that the argument focus item is out of its normal position in the clause, it is said to be FRONTED; the focus is thus positionally marked.[40] We can therefore think of a FRONTED POSITION which precedes the CORE of the clause (Van Valin 1993:5). Fronted items still take part in clause syntax; they retain case marking, for example. They may also have a pragmatic role other than focus: they may be topic, for instance, as in (52). Thus, fronting is commonly associated with prominence or saliency rather than with a particular pragmatic role.

In some languages, two elements can be fronted: the first is generally a salient topic, and the second an element in argument focus.

---

[39]More generally, expressions may be placed as far towards the (right) end of the sentence as the syntax of the language permits, in order for the intonation nucleus to fall on them (Firbas 1964). Such focused expressions, Firbas calls "rhemes".

[40]The fronting of focused constituents falls short of being an absolute universal, as claimed by Gundel (1988:231) and Givón (1990:727); Mambila and other Bantu languages constitute an exception (Perrin 1994).

(52) a. Mayan languages; here, Tz'utujil (verb-initial; Aissen
          1992:72, citing Dayley 1985)

Topic/Pt of Dep   —Focus—
Ja gáarsa   cheqe ch'uu' neeruutij
the heron   only fish eat
It's only fish that the heron eats.
[more literally, The heron, it's only fish that it eats.]

   b. Mbyá Guaraní (S V Complement; Dooley 1982:326)

—Topic—   —Focus—
yma-gua   kuery ma   mombyry ete   i-kuai
long.ago-NOM COLL boundary far   really 3-live.PL
The people of long ago, really far away they lived.

   c. Koiné Greek (VSO; Levinsohn 2000:37)

Topic[41] Focus
Su   pistin echeis
you   faith you.have

Topic Focus
kago: erga   echo:
and.I works I.have
You have faith, I have works. (James 2:18)

11.4 Overall structuring

The three types of articulation we have discussed (topic-comment,
presentational, focus-presupposition) are discourse-pragmatic configurations of the clause. We now consider some other elements that are important for discourse-pragmatic structuring; namely, dislocated elements
(Radford 1988:530–533). These occur outside the clause but within the
sentence. They are separated both phonologically and syntactically from
the clause, having their own intonation contours and, in some instances,
no case marking (Van Valin 1993:12ff).

LEFT-DISLOCATED ELEMENTS can include vocatives, short replies (Yes, No),
exclamations, and some points of departure (see section 11.4.1).
RIGHT-DISLOCATED ELEMENTS can include vocatives, tag questions, and tails
(see section 11.4.2). An overall scheme for the sentence, then, is displayed
in (53), adapted from Van Valin 1993 (see Dik 1978).

---

[41]The topics are contrastive; see section 11.5.

(53)

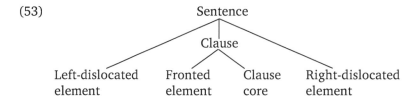

Dislocated elements are a type of adjunct, and more than one can occur in each position (Radford 1988:532f).

11.4.1 Point of departure. The term POINT OF DEPARTURE (Beneš 1962, cited in Garvin 1963:508) designates an initial element, often fronted or left-dislocated, which cohesively anchors the subsequent clause(s) to something which is already in the context (i.e., to something accessible in the hearer's mental representation).[42] It "sets a spatial, temporal, or individual domain within which the main predication holds" (Chafe 1976:50).[43] It is backward-looking, in the sense of locating the anchoring place within the existing mental representation, but is forward-looking in that it is the subsequent part of the sentence which is anchored in that place.

It was mentioned in section 7.4 that temporal and spatial points of departure in narrative commonly indicate the onset of thematic groupings. Examples (29) and (31) are repeated from that discussion.

(29)   —Temporal point of departure—
       So after waiting another two hours, it was finally announced,
       "Train…will be leaving…"

                                    (appendix B, line 19)

(31)   —Spatial pt of dep—
       About halfway there, there was some nice couple…

                                    (appendix B, line 59)

In (31), and possibly (29) as well, the clause following the point of departure is presentational. Points of departure and other left-dislocated elements commonly have their own intonation contour and a secondary sentence stress.

---

[42]The topic of a sentence may also provide a point of departure (Levinsohn 2000:10–11), whether it is left-dislocated or merely fronted (see below).

[43]Chafe (1987:36) uses the term "starting point" for this kind of element.

Example (54) is from Mandarin Chinese (Li and Thompson 1976:462). The initial noun phrase establishes an individual point of departure. The clause following 'those trees' has topic-comment articulation.

(54) Individual pt of dep —Topic— Comment
      Neì-xie shùmu   *shù-shen* *dà*
      those tree   tree-trunk big
      Those trees, the trunks are big.

Aissen (1992:47) uses the term EXTERNAL TOPIC for a left-dislocated noun phrase and INNER TOPIC for clause-internal topics. Under her analysis, 'those trees' in (54) is an external topic and 'tree-trunk' is either inner topic or subject. In the present treatment, external topics are one kind of point of departure.

Both point of departure and topic make reference to something which is currently accessible to the hearer, so as to anchor the clause (or clause core) at that place in the mental representation (Chafe 1987:37; Lambrecht 1994:162ff). In particular, a TOPIC (external or inner) is a pointer to an entity node, anchoring the rest of the utterance there (Linde 1979:345; Reinhart 1982:24). This is why the anchor point must be locatable, i.e., accessible. Note the accessibility of the temporal, spatial, and individual points of departure illustrated: *after waiting another two hours* in (29), *about half-way there* in (31), and *those trees* in (54). The accessibility of topics (and other points of departure) means that, in general, they will be definite or generic, rather than indefinite (Gundel 1988:231; Givón 1990:740). These and other similarities between topics and points of departure sometimes make it convenient for the two categories to be treated as one.[44]

This chapter deals with SENTENCE TOPIC rather than what is sometimes called DISCOURSE TOPIC or DISCOURSE THEME (Reinhart 1982:2). Notionally, a discourse topic is what a (section of) discourse is about, while a sentence topic is an entity that the speaker indicates that a particular sentence is about (Tomlin et al. 1997:85), if, in fact, the sentence has such. There can be discourse topics for different levels of discourse: thematic unit, episode, or the entire text (op. cit., 90); sentence topics, of course, are always associated with a particular sentence.

---

[44]"Topics share also many properties with 'scene-setting' expressions...that specify the spatial or temporal background for the sentence" (Reinhart 1982:169).

Formally, both kinds of topic are manifested by expressions or other structural features (possibly with zero manifestation) that make a reference.[45] There is this difference, however: a discourse topic, once introduced (activated), can retain its status with minimal linguistic reference (see chapters 10 and 16–18), without regard to syntactic structure. A sentence topic, on the other hand, must be indicated structurally as such, so as to indicate its distinctness from its associated comment. This structural distinction can be of different kinds. In linear arrangement, the sentence can consist of two parts, topic and comment, often with an intonation break between them, possibly with the interposition of a flexible-order element such as parenthetical material or a particle. A less obvious kind of structural distinction is available if we assume something like generative phrase structure, in which the subject is a primary, immediate constituent of the clause. Via this "deep structure" separation, a grammatical subject can be assumed to be sentence topic, provided it satisfies the cognitive criterion of referring to an accessible entity.

It can happen that the same element is both a discourse topic and a sentence topic. For example, a sentence topic which is linguistically salient may also be a discourse topic that is being introduced; on the other end of the scale, a grammatical subject which is an unstressed pronoun, affix or zero is almost certainly a discourse topic that is already activated. But a non-subject affix, unstressed pronoun or zero is more likely to indicate a discourse topic that is not a sentence topic. And a "new" sentence topic that is activated just for one sentence would not be a discourse topic except in a very minimal sense.

11.4.2 Tail. Tails are right-dislocated elements which are "meant to clarify or modify (some constituent contained in) the predication" (Dik 1978:153). Consider (55) from Dik.

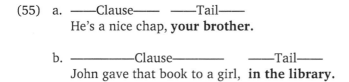

(55) a. ——Clause——   ——Tail——
          He's a nice chap, **your brother.**

      b. ————Clause————   ——Tail——
          John gave that book to a girl, **in the library.**

---

[45]By "discourse topic" or "global theme", some authors mean a proposition rather than a simple referent, specifically, a proposition which in some sense summarizes the discourse or section under consideration (van Dijk 1977:131ff; Brown and Yule 1983:68ff; Tomlin et al. 1997:83ff). In the present discussion, however, "discourse topics" are referential rather than propositional.

c. ————Clause————   —Tail——
John won't even be invited, eh... **Bill I mean.**

The tail in (55c) is a "repair device" and the one in (55b) may be an "after-thought". In many languages, however, noun phrase tails like (55a) are a regular, deliberate construction type (Givón 1990:760–762), and hence may represent a grammaticalization of final "repair" expressions. In Hixkaryana, noun phrase tails may have given rise, historically, to clause-final subjects that are clause-internal topics (Derbyshire 1985:103f).

(56)   ——Comment——   —Topic—
        kuraha yonyhoryeno **biryekomo**
        bow   he.made.it   **boy**
        The boy made a bow.

Even though tails have their own intonation contour (as with other right-dislocated elements), their stress is generally low-key.

11.5 Contrast

As was mentioned earlier, material in focus typically either (1) adds new information or (2) changes part of an already-activated propositional framework by replacement or by selecting between alternatives. Possibility (1) is illustrated in examples (42), (45), and (46). Possibility (2) involves CONTRAST.

A contrastive statement (which in this discussion will be labeled C) differs in one or more particulars from an already-activated propositional framework (labeled P). Contrast having just one point of difference with P is called SINGLE-DIFFERENCE CONTRAST; contrast with two (or more) points of difference is called DOUBLE- (or MULTIPLE-) DIFFERENCE CONTRAST (terminology adapted from Chafe 1976; the latter type corresponds to "parallel contrast" in Dik et al. 1981). In either type, a point of difference with P becomes the focus of C.

In SINGLE-DIFFERENCE CONTRAST, the one difference becomes the focus in C (Givón 1990:699) and is, in fact, narrow focus. Statement C may either replace the existing filler of a slot in P (e.g., to correct misinformation) or select between alternatives to fill an empty slot. In (47), repeated here, C replaces the filler of a slot in P.

(47)   I didn't say "èxcept", I said "Accept".

In (47), P is 'I said Xcept,' where X is a syllabic variable! The existing filler is the syllable *ex-;* the replacement is *ac-.* The particular intonation pattern in the first clause of (47) indicates anticipatory or TEMPORARY FOCUS (Levinsohn 2000:55–56).

In (57b), C selects between alternatives to fill an empty slot.

(57)   a. Was it my son or my daughter that killed the bear?
           ((P) 'X killed the bear;' X = 'my son' or 'my daughter'.)

       b. (C) Your DAUGHTER.

Note that C in (57) has, formally, the same narrow focus structuring as (48). Nevertheless, (48), an answer to the question "Who killed the bear?", is not contrastive; the underlying proposition has an empty slot but with no apparent list of alternatives in view. (57) makes a selection from an activated list of alternatives.[46]

In DOUBLE-DIFFERENCE CONTRAST, P has two slots that are already filled, and C supplies other fillers. One of the two points of difference with P is chosen as the focus of C; the other one is commonly taken as a topic or other point of departure and is generally given secondary stress, if not its own separate contour. (58) presents contiguous sentences from a Tzotzil (Mayan) text (Aissen 1992:49).

(58)   a. There was a man and a woman, newlyweds.

       b. The husband leaves, he goes, he travels.

       c. —Topic/Pt of Departure—   ————Comment————
           a   ti   antz-e   *jun = yo'on ta = xkom...*
           TOPIC DET woman-ENCLITIC   happily   stays
           The wife stays at home happily...

In this case, the two filled slots of the first proposition P are the subject 'the husband' and the predicate 'leaves, goes, travels'. P is verbalized as (58b), and, in this case, has the same topic-comment articulation as C (58c). The propositional framework common to P and C is 'X Y-ed'. In C, the X-difference becomes topic and the Y-difference becomes focus (here, comment). In both slots, C replaces the fillers that P had.

---

[46]The examples were chosen to be clear illustrations. In real life, activation states have fuzzy boundaries. Thus, the distinction between single-difference contrast and focus-presupposition with new information can be fuzzy, as well (see Givón 1990:703).

In double-difference contrast, proposition P need not have the same discourse-pragmatic configuration as C (Cruttenden 1986:91); in fact, as mentioned before, P need not be verbalized at all. Example (59) is line 3 of the text in Chafe 1987.

(59) I can recall...uh—...a big undergraduate class that I had.

In (59), "the speaker was contrasting his own understanding with that which had just been verbalized by the preceding speaker" (p. 27f). Proposition P may be thought of as something like 'You, the earlier speaker, have just recalled something from your college experience' (the actual words of P are not important, since it is probably not stored verbally). The two points of difference are 'you' versus 'I' and 'what you recalled' versus 'what I recall'; again, note replacement in each position.

11.6 Signals of overall structuring

Discourse-pragmatic structuring is interpreted partly by means of contextual evidence and partly by linguistic evidence. The present section focuses on linguistic evidence.

Intonational signals of focus and presupposition are largely predictable from the activation states of those elements: a focus has the intonational nucleus, while the presupposition component carries little or no stress. Dislocated elements, with their own intonation contours (and often secondary stress), are intermediate in phonological prominence, and their task of relocating a cohesive tie is intermediate in newsworthiness between focus and presupposition. Inner topics at times have their own contour and secondary stress, depending on their activation status.

One thing that separate contours do is indicate boundaries between constituents, and they are often accompanied by a pause. Pause can either be unfilled, or filled with morphemic material (Cruttenden 1986:36ff). A particular kind of pause filler is called a SPACER (Dooley 1990:477ff). Spacers tend to be short expressions with little or no stress, whose lexical meaning has sentence scope; they often indicate tense, aspect, or mode. They may have a default grammatical position in the sentence (e.g., after the verb or after the first word or phrase), but alternatively can be placed between constituents with distinct discourse-pragmatic roles. Their presence there helps to indicate the boundaries between these constituents. Often, the constituent that spacers follow is focus or topic/point of departure. Spacers from Mbyá Guaraní are illustrated in (60), particularly the modal particle *je* 'hearsay' (as in (41), CAPS signal the intonation nucleus and underlining signals secondary sentence stress).

(60) a. Men were discussing the fact that a hawk had told them not
          to enclose their chickens. They decided to do as he said.

    —Topic—   ——Comment——
    u<u>ru</u>   je   nha-mboty   eME
    chicken **hearsay** 1 + 2-enclose prohibitive
    As for the chickens, as he said, let's not enclose them!

      b. A group of Mbyá were making a long journey.

    —Focus—   —Presupposition—
    ka'aguy aNHO **tema je**   o-axa o-je'oivy
    woods only CONT **hearsay** 3-pass 3-go.plural
    It was only through woods, it is said, that they were passing.

      c. Our Father and his rival were on a journey. The rival went
          behind, while

    —Topic—   —Comment—
    nhande-<u>ru</u> **ma**   je   o-o tenoNDE
    1 + 2-father **boundary hearsay** 3-go ahead
    Our Father, it is said, went in front.

In (60a), the hearsay particle *je* occurs between the topic (a fronted direct
object *uru* 'chicken') and the comment. In (60b), *je* plus the aspect particle
tema 'CONTinuously' occurs between focus and presupposition. In (60c),
although all elements are in their basic order (SVO), the topic (subject) is
still highlighted as the point of departure in double-difference contrast by
spacers (*ma* 'boundary' plus *je*) and secondary stress. Note that the mean-
ings of *je* and *tema* say nothing about discourse-pragmatic structuring; it is
their positioning which indicates structural boundaries.

11.7 Marked versus unmarked structuring

Some discourse-pragmatic configurations are susceptible to a variety of
interpretations, hence become general-purpose, default constructions;
others are used only for specific discourse-pragmatic purposes. Constructions of the first kind are UNMARKED configurations, those of the second
kind are MARKED ones.[47] Unmarked configurations represent an "automatic

---

[47]It is common for marked configurations to be largely restricted to main clauses
(although Green (1976) notes that this can vary with language, construction type, and
discourse-pragmatic conditions). Thus, when morphosyntactic change enters the language
from discourse-pragmatics, it shows up first in main clauses and only later (if at all) in
subordinate clauses.

pilot" mode of information transfer: consecutive bits of information are being added to the mental representation in routine, predictable ways. Marked configurations represent a more "hands-on" approach, being used when information transfer becomes nonroutine. Perhaps the incoming information is to be added at a new place in the mental representation; perhaps the speaker suspects that some faulty idea has slipped into the representation and needs to be corrected, etc. (see Givón 1982).

It has often been claimed that, cross-linguistically, topic-comment articulation is the unmarked configuration (see Lambrecht 1994:126). Recent studies, however, have turned up languages for which that may not be the case: Ojibwa (Tomlin and Rhodes 1979), Ute (Givón 1983:141–214), Seneca (Chafe 1985a), and others (see Payne 1992:6). In some of these languages, focus-presupposition (in that order) seems to be the most common configuration.

Mithun (1987) claims that this difference is due to a more fundamental distinction. Some languages, such as English, are SYNTACTICALLY BASED: their clause constituents tend to be ordered according to grammatical rules, with real-time extragrammatical motivations surfacing only rarely. (These are also known as fixed or rigid word order languages.) For such languages, Mithun (p. 325) finds that the unmarked configuration is indeed topic-comment, with subject as topic; hence, the unmarked topic-comment configuration is subject-predicate in subject-initial languages which are syntactically based. Other configurations are marked ones, being used only for special purposes. Marked structurings in these languages include focus-presupposition and presentational. They also include what she calls MARKED TOPIC-COMMENT, in which the topic is indicated linguistically as being the point of departure. This can happen, for example, by fronting, as in (61).

(61) Topic/Pt of Dep ——Comment——
      The *bear,* your   DAUGHTER killed.

In (61), the topic/point of departure *the bear* is direct object. The comma signals an intonation break (i.e., the topic is left-dislocated), which is common for this configuration.

In languages in which the topic/point of departure is already sentence initial, it may be marked with a separate intonation contour, secondary stress, and spacers (60c). Marked topic constructions are reserved for either double-difference contrast (see above) or a change in subtopics within an already-established referential field; both uses involve node-switching (Aissen 1992:76f). For marked topics, the order topic-comment is cross-linguistically normative, reflecting the fact that the topic is also the point of departure.

In PRAGMATICALLY BASED (free or flexible word order) languages, the order of clause constituents is less often motivated by purely syntactic conditions, but is highly responsive to discourse-pragmatic factors. In this type of language, it may be questioned whether an unmarked, neutral configuration exists. The most likely candidate is quite often one in which constituents "appear in descending order of newsworthiness" (Mithun, 1987:325), e.g., when focus-presupposition occurs in that order.

All of the pragmatically based languages studied by Mithun have verb agreement for all subcategorized arguments, and the verb often occurs alone as a clause. In languages in which there is verb agreement for only some of these arguments or the verb does not occur alone, constituent order may not be as flexible (pp. 324f).

11.8 Discourse function of configurations

Although it is becoming clear that languages differ along the lines noted by Mithun, it is also becoming apparent that certain correspondences between discourse-pragmatic configurations and discourse functions are highly predictable across languages. Some correlations that have highly universal status are summarized in (62) (Andrews 1985; Gundel 1988; Givón 1990).

(62) Configurations	Common discourse functions
point of departure	onset of thematic groupings double-difference contrast
unmarked topic + comment	maintaining established topic
marked topic/point of departure + comment	switch in subtopics double-difference contrast
presentational	introduction of prominent entities
focus + presupposition	single-difference contrast adding a new item of information to a given framework
tail	clarification, afterthought

Key Concepts:
discourse-pragmatic structuring of sentences
focus
    scope of focus
        with topic-comment articulation: predicate focus or comment
           within comment: focus proper
        with presentational articulation: argument or sentence focus
        with focus-presupposition articulation:
           argument focus
           marked focus
           cleft sentence
topic
    discourse topic
    sentence topic
pragmatic role
overall positions in sentence
    left dislocated—fronted-clause core—right dislocated
point of departure
    external topic
    preposed adverbial expressions
tail
contrast
    single-difference contrast
    double-difference contrast
marked versus unmarked structuring
    marked topic/point of departure-comment
type of information under focus: new versus contrastive
spacers
syntactically-based versus pragmatically-based languages
    fixed/rigid word order languages
    free/flexible word order languages
common discourse functions of configurations

12

Foreground and Background Information

12.1 Foreground and background

Visualize someone pouring water onto an uneven surface. Sometimes it will temporarily build up without much spreading, then suddenly it will break out and flow. Similar things happen with mental representations. Some passages in a text may comment on something that already took place, prepare the hearer for something that is to come, or provide auxiliary information on something that is being mentioned. In such places, a section of the mental representation is being filled out or consolidated, without major new sections being added. Other passages will expand the mental representation in new directions.

The terms FOREGROUND and BACKGROUND describe parts of a text which, respectively, do or do not extend the basic framework of the mental representation. If only the foreground were available, the resulting representation might be complete in its general outline, but would be sketchy. Background aids in internal and external contextualization (see section 5.2).

Foreground and background have linguistic correlates. Hopper and Thompson (1980:252) identify a range of morphosyntactic devices with different degrees of TRANSITIVITY (using the term in a broader sense than having a direct object). These are presented in the following table. High transitivity correlates with foreground in narrative, low transitivity with background.

(63) Scale of transitivity of a clause (A = agent, O = object)

Type	High transitivity	Low transitivity
Participants	2 or more, A & O *I saw the man*	1 participant *I fell*
Kinesis	action *I hugged Sally*	non-action *I like Sally*
Aspect	telic *I ate it up*	atelic *I am eating it*
Punctuality	punctiliar *I kicked it*	durative *I carried it*
Volitionality	volitional *I wrote your name*	non-volitional *I forgot your name*
Affirmation	affirmative *I did it*	negative *I didn't do it*
Mode	realis *I did it*	irrealis *I would do it*
Agency	A high in potency *George startled me*	A low in potency *The picture startled me*
Affectedness of O	O totally affected *I drank the milk*	O not totally affected *I drank some of the milk*
Individuation of O	O highly individuated *Fritz drank the beer*	O non-individuated *Fritz drank some beer*

Consider (64) (from Hopper and Thompson 1980:253).

(64) a. Jerry likes beer.
      b. Jerry knocked Sam down.

(64b) is much higher in transitivity than (64a) because it has action kinesis, telic aspect,[48] and punctuality, while the O *(Sam)* is totally affected and is high in individuation (i.e., is referential, animate, and a proper noun). Because of this, Hopper and Thompson predict that (64b) is much more likely than (64a) to occur as foreground.

Nevertheless, although there appears to be a general correlation between transitive morphosyntax and foreground information in narrative,

---

[48]Telic (or completive) aspect presents an event as having "a clear terminal point" (Crystal 1997:347).

the correlation between any single parameter and foregrounding is only partial; the relationship with grounding may be indirect, correlating more closely with other factors (DeLancey 1987:54f).[49]

12.2 Events

The foreground-background distinction offers a binary choice. Grimes 1975 provides finer distinctions, at least for narrative. "The first distinction made in the analysis of discourse is between events and nonevents" (1975:35); this is a way of talking about foreground versus background which applies specifically to narrative.[50] An EVENT is an action or happening which extends the basic structure of the mental representation. It is presented as happening at a particular time and place, and is generally told in temporal sequence with other events.[51] In appendix A, events include *the garage door opened* (line 7), *suddenly the room went black* (line 13), and *Pattie swept the children into her arms* (line 15).

Events in a narrative make up what is sometimes called the EVENT LINE (story line, main line, time line). The event line is the foreground, the basic framework for internal contextualization.

It is sometimes useful to distinguish between two kinds of events, here referred to as primary and secondary (following Huisman 1973). In general, PRIMARY EVENTS have greater informational salience and SECONDARY ones have less. More specific differences will depend on the language. In Angaataha, for instance, this distinction is marked on the verb (op. cit. 30f). In many languages, however, the distinction is not made systematically.[52]

12.3 Nonevents

Nonevents are of various types. Grimes (1975) lists six: participant orientation, setting, explanation,[53] evaluation, discourse irrealis, and performative information. These categories are not always mutually exclusive; bits of information in a text can belong to more than one, having more than

[49]Callow (1974:56) notes a further complication: "Material which might have a background function in narrative may be thematic in...other types of discourse." For discussion of this point, see Levinsohn 2000:169.

[50]Other terminology sometimes used for this distinction is thematic versus nonthematic, primary versus secondary, backbone versus support.

[51]Definitions of foreground in narrative tend either to emphasize a strict temporal sequence of telling (Thompson 1987) or notions of importance and salience (Dry 1992).

[52]Summary statements, whether at the beginning or the end of a thematic grouping, may be secondary events or nonevents. Either way, they are generally presented as background information.

[53]Grimes actually refers to this as *background information,* but the use of that term here would be confusing, since background here is a broader notion.

one discourse function. Quite often, different kinds of information are mixed
together in a single utterance, particularly in tightly crafted written material.

PARTICIPANT ORIENTATION has the purpose of introducing, reintroducing,
or describing participants. Participant orientation may be given before its
relevance to the story is clear. For major participants, it often comes first.
Expressions of participant orientation in appendix A include *Pattie Uridel,
36* (line 1), and *her job as an insurance executive in Aurora, Ill.* (line 2). See
chapters 16–18 for further discussion of participant reference.

SETTING information indicates the time, place, or circumstances under
which events take place. Again from appendix A, examples include *The afternoon sky was darkening by the minute* (line 1), and *Black clouds were
sweeping in* (line 2). In such statements we note that setting often goes beyond the more obvious kinds of circumstances "to encompass the psychological climate that anticipates a beginning narrative event" (Ochs
1997:196).

EXPLANATION or comment clarifies what is happening, and possibly why
(this can relate to either internal or external contextualization). Sometimes,
happenings may be told as background, especially if out of temporal sequence with the events per se. Thus, in appendix A, the sentence *Jimmy, ten,
was visiting friends* (line 11) explains *Three of the four Uridel children* in line 10.

EVALUATION is an expression of external contextualization: "the point of
the narrative,...why it was told, and what the narrator is getting at"
(Labov 1972:366). Alternatively, it may tell how the speaker feels about
just one item. Evaluation can be either DIRECT, in which the narrator will,
so to speak, "stop the narrative, turn to the listener, and tell him what the
point is" (p. 371), or INDIRECT, attributed to a participant in the text world,
through words or actions. Indirect evaluation is more subtle, hence often
more effective. Appendix A is full of indirect evaluation: *You could jump
up and touch them, she thought* (line 3), *mother and children clung desperately
to one another* (line 16), etc.

DISCOURSE IRREALIS (which Grimes calls *collateral information*) mentions
what does not happen, or what could possibly happen, as a means of highlighting what actually does happen. Common forms of irrealis are nega-
tion *(such-and-such did not happen)* and possible outcomes. The latter
category includes questions *(could she escape?)*, desires/plans *(he wanted
to escape),* and conflict/obstacles *(the rope wouldn't let him escape).* Possible outcomes provide strong cohesive ties pointing forward in the text:
the hearer's interest is aroused to find out which actually happens and
how. In Appendix A, possible outcomes include *She considered staying in
the car* (line 7) and *I can't hold on!* (line 20).

PERFORMATIVE INFORMATION (Grimes, chapter 5) deals with aspects of the situation under which the text is produced, especially the speaker-hearer axis. This comes out when the speaker speaks in first person to the hearer in second person. Also included in this category are morals, conclusions, and applications to the audience, which also overlap with evaluation.

12.4 Signals of kinds of information

Correlations between linguistic signals and kinds of information, even though partial, are valuable to the analyst. Here we consider aspect, subordination, and reported conversation.

ASPECT is represented in Hopper and Thompson's list in the table in (63), and its relation to discourse is further dealt with in Hopper 1982. "In PERFECTIVE aspect...a situation is seen as a whole, regardless of the time contrasts which may be a part of it...IMPERFECTIVE...draws attention to the internal time-structuring of the situation" (Crystal 1997:283). In appendix A, note the verbs with imperfective aspect: *The afternoon sky was darkening* (line 1), *Black clouds were sweeping* (line 2), *who'd been stowing away patio furniture* (line 8), *Jimmy...was visiting friends* (line 11). Note the imperfective (progressive) aspect of *was darkening* (line 1) as compared to the perfective aspect of *went black* (line 13); the former is background, the latter is foreground even though, semantically, the states of affairs are very similar.

SUBORDINATE CLAUSES most frequently present background information (Givón 1984:314; Thompson 1987); main clauses can present background or foreground. This picture is somewhat complicated by two facts: (1) "many languages do not make a clear morphosyntactic distinction between coordinate and subordinate constructions" (Givón 1990:848), and (2) post-nuclear subordinate clauses can encode foreground (Thompson 1987:451). Consider postposed *as*-clauses in appendix A: *as Pattie Uridel, 36, drove home* (line 1), *as she pulled into her driveway* (line 5), *as the roof shot from the house* (line 15); certainly the last two are foreground. In English, postposed *as*- and *when*-clauses commonly provide information that is at least as salient as that of the preceding main clause (Levinsohn 1992).[54]

In REPORTED CONVERSATION, three things need to be considered: the act of speaking, the speech content, and the event being talked about. The act of speaking may or may not be an event (see section 14.2), while the content is often some type of nonevent. This is seen in appendix A, line 22: *I'm not giving up my kids, she vowed.* The act of speech is an event (note the

---

[54]Bolinger (1977:517) does not treat such clauses as subordinate.

perfective aspect); the content is discourse irrealis, a possible outcome. (In some languages, acts of quoted irrealis are signaled as secondary events.) The event being talked about (here, the foreshadowed outcome) is usually a primary event, but its actual realization may be implicit. In appendix A, nothing in the text explicitly says that Pattie did not give up her kids (lines 20–21 come close). On a smaller scale, quotations such as *"Let's go downstairs"* (line 12) are often intended to imply, in the absence of signals to the contrary, that the spoken-of event actually took place at that time (Grimes 1975:69f).

12.5 Markedness in grounding

Typically, the body of a text is UNMARKED for prominence. Thus, the story line or foreground events of a narrative do not normally carry a marker. Some sentences, however, may be MARKED as conveying information of special importance; in other words, they are highlighted. Similarly, other sentences may be marked as background information—they convey information of secondary importance.

The HIGHLIGHTING of an utterance is usually because of its importance to how a narrative "comes out" or to its evaluation. Linguistic signals are used to indicate highlighted status. Fronted expressions in Appendix A such as *suddenly* (line 13) can indicate a highlighted episode, as can other emotive words within such an episode (*groaning* (line 14), *desperately* (line 16), *cried out* (line 17), etc.). In many languages, a full noun phrase can be used to highlight a key event (Levinsohn 2000:140).

A clause can be signaled as background when, without such marking, it would be interpreted as foreground. The conjunction *whereas* does this in English, although it is not used widely in narrative. Koiné Greek has a similar element, *mén,* which occurs in narrative, and which can indicate that an action is backgrounded with respect to following events (Levinsohn 2000:170–171).

Key Concepts:
foreground versus background
transitivity
kinds of information in narrative
    events
        primary versus secondary events
    nonevents
        participant orientation
        setting
        explanation
        evaluation
           direct versus indirect
        discourse irrealis
        performative information
signals of kinds of information
    perfective versus imperfective aspect
    subordinate clauses
    reported conversation
highlighting

13

Signaling Relations Between Propositions

*I grant you it's easy enough to choose between a 'but' and an
'and.' It's a bit more difficult between 'and' and 'then.' But defi-
nitely the hardest thing may be to know whether one should put
an 'and' or leave it out.*

Albert Camus, *The Plague*

Teachers of composition have traditionally counseled writers to organize their work around a framework of propositions, hierarchically arranged. The higher levels of the framework then serve as summaries of
what we have been calling thematic groupings; presumably, if the hierarchy is elaborated in detail, its lowest levels will correspond closely to individual sentences and clauses of the text. A PROPOSITION can be thought of
as the semantic counterpart of a clause (see Crystal 1997:313).

Propositions comprising the content framework of a discourse are related, not only in a hierarchy (as we would find in an outline), but also by
specific SEMANTIC RELATIONS. Consider (65), a short text from *Scientific
American,* along with an analysis of its semantic relations from Mann and
Thompson (1987:13ff).

(65) Title: Dioxin

    a. Concern that this material is harmful to health or the environment may be misplaced.
    b. Although it is toxic to certain animals,
    c. evidence is lacking that it has any serious long-term effect on human beings.
    d. Analysis:

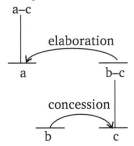

Diagram (65d) can be read as follows. Propositions *b* and *c* form a unit that is an elaboration of *a*. Proposition *b*, in turn, is a concession to *c*. Whereas concession in (65) is coded explicitly by *although,* the relation of elaboration is implicit: no linguistic material occurs that means 'elaboration'. Yet the existence of some kind of semantic relation between *a* and the unit *b–c* is implied by the juxtaposition of these sentences.

Among the different listings and categories of semantic relations that have been proposed are those found in Beekman, Callow, and Kopesec 1981; Grimes 1975; Hobbs 1985; Larson 1984; Longacre 1996, chapter 3; and Mann and Thompson 1987. The interested reader should at least skim one of these treatments.

In some of these, an attempt is made to incorporate a feature of relative prominence. Mann and Thompson (1987:31f), for example, observe that in many relations

> one member of the pair [the nucleus] is more essential to the writer's purpose than the other [the satellite]....If units that only function as satellites and never as nuclei are deleted, we should still have a coherent text with a message resembling that of the original; it should be something like a synopsis of the original text.

Thus, the arrows in (65d) indicate that what is being elaborated (proposition *a*) is more essential than the elaboration *(b–c)*, and what is being conceded to *(c)* is more important than the concession *(b)*. Prominence of this kind appears to be closely related to the foreground-background distinction discussed in section 12.1.

13.1 The preferred order of propositions in VO and OV languages

In a landmark study, Greenberg (1963) showed that there is a correlation between the normal order of certain pairs of grammatical elements and the normal order of verb and object. For example, if the object usually follows the verb (VO), then the language tends to have *pre*positions, auxiliary verbs before the main verb, and noun heads before modifying relative clauses. If the object usually precedes the verb (OV), on the other hand, then the language tends to have *post*positions, auxiliary verbs after the main verb, and noun heads after modifying relative clauses.[55]

Roberts (1997) found that this correlation extends to the order of propositions that are in a relationship of "unequal natural prominence" (p. 20). In prototypical VO languages, the preferred order is for the more prominent proposition to be given first, whereas, in prototypical OV languages, the opposite order is preferred.[56] For example, it is normal in VO languages for a reason clause to follow the main proposition it supports, but to precede the main proposition in OV languages. Similarly, when a positive assertion is supported by a negative statement, the negative proposition tends to follow the positive one in VO languages, but precede it in OV languages. These preferences are illustrated by comparing line 27 of appendix B in English with how it would likely come out in an OV language:

(66) VO main proposition: Which we decided we would do
        positive reason: since we wanted to get to Omaha
        negative reason: and not stay in Minneapolis all night in the train station.

     OV negative reason: We wanted not to stay in Minneapolis all night in the train station
        positive reason: but get to Omaha,
        main proposition: so we decided we would do that.

---

[55]For refinements to Greenberg's conclusions, see Dryer 1992.

[56]In a prototypical VO language, head constituents consistently precede non-heads; in a prototypical OV language, head constituents consistently follow non-heads. See also Levinsohn 1999. Even in prototypical OV languages, however, it is not unusual for adverbial clauses of purpose to follow the proposition to which they are subordinated (Greenberg 1963 and Shin Ja Hwang, pers. com.).

Typically, when the preferred order of propositions is followed, the semantic relationship between them may be left implicit, whereas, if the language permits the order of propositions to be reversed, then the relationship has to be made explicit. In the original, VO version of (66), for example, when the positive reason is followed by the negative one, the default conjunction *and* is used (see further below). When the order is reversed in the OV version, *but* is used.

13.2 Some constraints on semantic relations

When semantic relations are not coded explicitly and completely, clues are often furnished which help narrow down the range of possible interpretations (Blakemore 1987 and 1992, chapter 8). Four clues are now considered: intonation, the order of elements, expectation structures, and morphemic signals. (These are beyond the intonational and syntactic signals—including juxtaposition—that merely imply that some kind of semantic relation is intended.)

Some patterns of INTONATION indicate specific relations, others fit a broad range of interpretations. Read the following sentences with rising intonation on the first clause and falling on the second.

(67) a. Head 'em up, move 'em out! (sequence)
      b. No shoes, no service! (condition)
      c. All for one, one for all! (association)

Thus, a rising intonation pattern is compatible with sequence, condition, and association relations, but does not encode any of them directly.

The ORDER OF ELEMENTS may also suggest an interpretation. For example, Healey and Healey (1990:224) noted the following correlation for Koiné Greek between the ordering of adverbial ("circumstantial") subordinate clauses with respect to their main clauses: those clauses that appeared to express temporal and most logical relations occurred before the main clause in 86 percent of instances. In turn, those clauses that appeared to express elaboration relations and the logical relations of result-means and reason-result occurred following their main clause in 79 percent of instances. Thus, order can help to narrow down the range of possible semantic relations.

In addition, EXPECTATION STRUCTURES (section 9.4) will suggest "off the shelf" interpretations for semantic relations, just as for other aspects of communication. Consider appendix A, line 7: *She considered staying in the car, but the garage door opened and the husky figure of her husband, Jim, appeared.* From the "suburbia" schema, it seems likely that Jim opened the garage door *in order for* Pattie to drive in and thus be able to get out of the car and into the house where it would be safer (line 9). In other words, what Jim did enabled a subsequent act by Pattie. If so, then it is due to a culture-specific expectation structure that enablement can be interpreted here; houses are not safer than cars everywhere.

13.3 Connectives

The most obvious kind of clue constraining the interpretation of a semantic relation over against another is morphemic. This is often a connective, such as a CONJUNCTION.

Connectives may signal very specific semantic relations, such as concession—conveyed in (65b) by the conjunction *although*. Often, however, they only provide a general semantic pointer to the relation, leaving the hearer to deduce a more specific relation with the help of the context.

Such is the case with *because,* which is used six times in appendix B. Sometimes it introduces the direct cause of the event described in the previous clause (lines 17, 21, 43). Sometimes it introduces the reason for an action (42, 61). It may even introduce the means of doing an action (28). The presence of *because* itself, however, only constrains the hearer to interpret what follows as STRENGTHENING what has just been said.

Similarly, *but* (15, 26, 30, 40, 42, 52, 57) provides a general pointer that what follows COUNTERS some expectation created by a previous proposition or group of propositions, but does not signal any more specific relation such as antithesis, concession, contrast (see Blakemore 1987 and 1992, section 8.3).

13.3.1 Associatives. Some connectives signal little if any semantic relation between propositions. When *and* links propositions in English, for instance, it says nothing about the semantic relation between them. This is seen in the sentences of (68), where possible semantic relations between the propositions concerned are indicated in parentheses.

(68) a. I like her, **and** she likes me. (reciprocity)
      b. I hit her, **and** she hit me. (sequence)
      c. She apologized, **and** now I'm happy. (result)

In (68), the semantic relations in parentheses are plausible interpretations, given the content. However, they are not actually encoded by *and* (Blakemore 1987:111ff).

Nevertheless, *and* does contain a specific instruction to the hearer: ASSOCIATE these propositions together! In other words, *and* is a PRAGMATIC CONNECTIVE (op. cit.) that constrains the hearer to process together the material thus associated.

13.3.2 Additives. Some ADDITIVE connectives instruct the hearer to find a PARALLEL PROPOSITION to which to append the current one (see the use of *ma* 'also' in sentences 6 and 8 of the Tyap text given in appendix C). Often, these propositions are not contiguous (see the use of *again* in line 57 of appendix B, which describes an event parallel to that of line 22). What is different from the first proposition, can be expected to be (in) the focus of the second one.

Some languages are very specific as to what is to be added to what. This may be indicated by the position of the additive.[57] Alternatively, the language may use distinct additives if a different subject or a different predicate is to be appended. In such languages, one additive (indicated here by +) would be used in *Bill has a computer. Susan + has one,* whereas another one would be used in *Bill is good at sports. He is + a good linguist.* See Spreda 1984 for other distinctions found between additives.

It is not unusual for an additive to be used not only when a parallel proposition is to be found, but also when a contradictory proposition is appended. The pragmatic effect produced when this happens is that of CONCESSION, as in *He saw the man lying at the side of the road. + He didn't stop to help.*

Additives are also used in some languages to CONFIRM a previous proposition. The examples in (69) are from Blass 1990 and Follingstad 1994; for each connective, an English gloss is given in parentheses.

(69)   a.   He told her to do it.
            + ('and so') she did it.[58]

       b.   A: Zimpeale is a Dagaati.
            B: + ('indeed') he is; I know him.

       c.   He doesn't want to stop.
            + ('even') not for a little while.

---

[57]In Koiné Greek, adverbial *kaí* constrains the constituent that immediately follows it to be added to a corresponding constituent of a previous clause or sentence (Levinsohn 2000:100).

[58]See sentence 13 of appendix C.

Finally, additives are sometimes used instead of associative conjunctions to append information of UNEQUAL IMPORTANCE. Examples of this are discussed in appendix C (see also Levinsohn 2000:108–109).

13.3.3 Developmental markers. Whereas connectives like *and* and some additives instruct the hearer to associate information together, some conjunctions convey the opposite and constrain the reader to *move on to the next point.* We will call these connectives DEVELOPMENTAL MARKERS because they indicate that the material so marked represents a new development in the story or argument, as far as the author's purpose is concerned.[59]

Particularly in SOV languages that permit several subordinate clauses to precede the main verb,[60] a developmental marker is often attached to the end of a subordinate clause to (act as a spacer and) mark the transition to the development described in the next clause. The absence of the marker, or its replacement by an additive, indicates that the same point is still being developed. In the first sentence of a story in the Suruwahá (Arawá) language of Brazil, for instance, the developmental marker (DM) *na* is added to those clauses that lead to the next development.

(70)   I planted the field and
        because the sun was hot,
        instead of lying down + DM
        I bathed in the river and
        I returned;
        before I lay down + DM
        it thundered.

In (70), the development marker marks *I bathed in the river* and *it thundered* as the next developments in the story.

A developmental marker may also be attached to sentence introducers, to indicate that the sentence concerned represents a new development in the story or argument. It may also be attached to references to participants, to indicate that the next development(s) will involve the participant concerned (see Levinsohn 1976).[61] Both of these uses are illustrated

---

[59]Information brought in with a developmental marker "is relevant in its own right" (Blass 1993).

[60]Longacre (1985:263ff) calls such constructions "chaining structures". They often have markers of "switch reference" (Andrews 1985:115), i.e., indicators of whether the subject (or, more rarely, topic) of the clause concerned is the same as or different from that of a later clause.

[61]Developmental markers may also be attached to preposed topics (points of departure) when a background comment ("digression") about the topic is to be made (op. cit.).

in the following extract from a folktale in the Inga (Quechuan) language of Colombia (see Longacre and Levinsohn 1978:112—the developmental marker *ka* occurs at the end of the subordinate clause or noun phrase concerned).

(71) 1. At that time   the mother-   went ahead, weeping, to
                            in-law + DM   where she had buried the
                                               piece of fruit.

      2. Arriving + DM (she)   said, 'Here is where the child
                                            is buried.'

      3. Having said   (she)   fled to go hang herself.
          that + DM

      4. At that time   the father + DM dug up the grave.

      5. On removing   (he)   found just a piece of fruit.
          the earth

      6.   (He)   said, 'Oh no! Now it's clear
                                            to me.'

      7. Having-said   (he)   followed her trail.
          that + DM

In (71), the attachment of the developmental marker to the subjects (lines 1, 4) indicates that the next developments in the story will be actions performed by the mother-in-law and the father, respectively. In lines 2 and 3, the developmental markers separate the preceding background material from the following new developments (foreground material). Notice the absence of the developmental marker in line 5. This constrains the finding of the piece of fruit not to be viewed as a new development (perhaps because the hearers already know what will be found), but as part of the same "development unit" (Levinsohn 2000:275) as line 4 (and 6).

Developmental markers in VO languages have been found to be either conjunctions (e.g., *de* in Greek; Levinsohn 2000:72) or particles associated with the verb phrase. Appendix C presents an extract from a text in the Tyap language of Nigeria in which both the developmental marker *(kàn)* and two additive markers *(kìn, ma)* occur between the subject and the main verb.

Typically, developmental markers are not used in a narrative until the scene has been set. See appendix C for an extensive introduction before the first instance of the developmental marker is found.

Key Concepts:
proposition
semantic relations between propositions
preferred order of propositions in VO and OV languages
constraints on semantic relations
    intonation
    relative order of the clauses
    expectation structures
morphemic signals (e.g., conjunctions)
    strengthening
    countering
pragmatic connectives
    associatives
    additives
        parallelism
        concession
        confirmation
        highlighting/backgrounding
    developmental markers

14

The Reporting of Conversation

"What is the use of a book", thought Alice, "without pictures or conversations?"

Lewis Carroll, *Alice in Wonderland*

Reported conversations tend not to be structured like ordinary narrative events. For example, references to a speaker who was previously the addressee may not follow the coding rules for other changes of subject (see chapter 17). It is common, too, for the verb used to introduce reported speech to be in the imperfective, rather than the perfective, or not to be conjugated at all.

First, though, some terminology!

A SPEECH ORIENTER is an expression which indicates who is speaking to whom.[62] Depending on the language and other factors, speech orienters may occur before the speech (e.g., *And finally, they told us, "The train is late."*—appendix B, line 11), after the speech (e.g., *"Tornado!" Pattie screamed*—appendix A, line 18), both before and after the speech, or even in the middle of the speech *("Mom!" cried Gregory, "I can't hold on!"*—appendix A, line 20). The orienter may also be omitted, as in lines 12–13 of appendix B.

The term CLOSED CONVERSATION refers to one in which each new speaker and addressee is drawn from the speakers and addressees of previous speeches of that conversation. Passage (72), a translation of part of a text in the Mofu-Gudur language of Cameroon (Pohlig and Levinsohn 1994:89), is

---

[62]Longacre (1996:89) uses the term "quotation formula". Other terms found include "speech margin", "quotation margin", and "quote tag". Speech orienters may also occur with the verbalization of a thought, as in sentence 3 of appendix A.

an example of a closed conversation; the stranger and the children address each other in turn.

(72) a. He said to them, "Children, what are you doing?"
      b. "We are sitting here guarding," answered the children.
      c. "What are you guarding?"
      d. "We are guarding sheep and goats."
      e. They asked the stranger, "Are you a thief?"
      f. "Ah! Am I a man who would steal from children?"

Passage (73) (from later in the same text) is an example of a conversation that is *not* closed, since the addressee of the second speech (the husband) was not the previous speaker (the stranger).

(73) a. The stranger said, "Please give me the foot (of the
         goat)! I will only crunch it; I won't eat it...as I haven't eaten
         for three days."
      b. The woman said to her husband, "Give him it, then!"

Speech orienters are affected by whether the conversation is closed or not. Once the participants in a closed Mofu-Gudur conversation have been established, for instance, the speech orienters may be omitted until the direction of the conversation is changed, as happens in sentence (72e). At the point where a conversation ceases to be closed, however, as in (73b), a speech orienter has to be used.

14.1 The presentation of speech

A basic distinction in the way speech is reported is between DIRECT SPEECH, INDIRECT SPEECH, and SEMIDIRECT SPEECH. In direct speech (e.g., *John said, "I can see you"*), the speaker is referred to with a first person pronoun and the addressee with a second person pronoun. In indirect speech (e.g., *John said he could see her*), references to the speaker and addressee are indirect: with a third person pronoun or, in the case of the speaker, with a LOGOPHORIC PRONOUN, i.e., one that refers to the speaker (Perrin 1974, Anderson and Keenan 1985:302–304).[63] In semidirect speech, one of the references is direct and one, indirect. For example, it is common in languages of West Africa for the reference to the addressee to be direct, but for the reference to the speaker to use a logophoric pronoun (LOG), as in *John said LOG can see you.*

---

[63]In indirect speech in English, the tense of the reported speech is often changed, too. In the example cited, *can* has been changed to *could.*

The use of direct versus indirect speech may be related to the speaker's *purpose* in referring to the speech, in particular, whether he or she wishes the hearer to believe that the message being reported is given verbatim or not. Li (1986:38ff) says that, by using direct speech in European languages, "the reporter-speaker intends for the hearer to believe that the form, the content and the nonverbal messages such as gestures and facial expressions of the reported speech originate from the reported speech." In indirect speech, on the other hand, "the reporter-speaker may communicate his own feelings through the form (e.g., intonation) and nonverbal messages of the reported speech as a comment on the content of the reported speech."

In some languages, factors that determine whether a reported speech is direct or indirect are basically *syntactic:*

- certain sentence types such as questions may have to be reported as direct speech
- speeches reported in subordinate clauses may have to be given in indirect or semidirect speech
- if the speaker or addressee is referred to in the speech, it may have to be reported in indirect or semidirect form.

In other languages, the way the speech is reported is determined by *discourse-pragmatic* factors, such as:

- the **prominence** of the speech. In Bafut (Cameroon), for instance, the default way of reporting speech is in semidirect form. Direct speech is used for highlighting, while the indirect form is reserved for speeches of a background nature (Mfonyam 1994:195).
- the relative **status** of the participants. The pronouncements of particularly important participants ("VIPs"—chapter 17) are given in direct speech, and those of other participants in indirect or semidirect speech.
- an approaching **climax.** In languages which normally use an orienter with reported speech, for instance, a shift to drama (i.e., with the orienters omitted) often occurs in the build-up to a climax (Longacre 1996:43).

14.2 The type of information of reported conversation

Typically, in narratives, reported conversations are not an end in themselves, but point forward to the nonspeech events which form the foreground of the story. Furthermore, if a reported conversation consists of several speeches, they are often not treated as the equivalent of that many individual events. This may be reflected in the speech orienters in at least three ways (more than one of which may be used at the same time).

- The verb of the speech orienter may be in the imperfective aspect or take some other marker that elsewhere tends to correlate with *backgrounded information* (chapter 12).
- Developmental markers (chapter 13) may be attached to descriptions of nonverbal events, but not normally be found in speech orienters. In other words, the reported speeches may not be treated as new developments in the narrative.
- Especially in oral texts, reported speeches may be grouped into *adjacency pairs* consisting of an initiating move and a resolving move (chapter 1). The most common pairs consist of a question plus an answer, a remark plus an evaluation, and a proposal plus its (often nonverbal) implementation[64] (loc. cit.). In some languages, such adjacency pairs may begin with a pre-speech orienter and end with a post-speech orienter, as in the question-answer pair in (74):

(74)   I asked, "What time is it?" (IM)
       "It's four o'clock," he replied. (RM)

Alternatively, reported speeches may be treated as foreground events. This is particularly evident in the reporting of what are essentially speech happenings, such as arguments, debates, and trials.

14.3 Changes of direction in reported conversations

Sometimes, instead of taking up the same topic as that of the previous speech and developing the conversation from the point at which the last speaker left off, the new speaker may change the direction of the conversation with a countering move (chapter 1). Such counters generally are marked in some way.

In Koiné Greek, for instance, the verb *apokrínomai*, which is usually glossed 'answer', typically signals a change of direction in a reported conversation. This is illustrated in (75), reflecting Acts 9:10–14; (75d) reports an objection to the instruction (proposal) of (75c).

(75)   a. The Lord said to him in a vision, "Ananias."
       b. He said, "Here I am, Lord."

---

[64]Longacre's term for this last adjacency pair is "proposal-response" or "proposal-execution".

    c. The Lord said to him, "Rise and go to the street called
       Straight, and at the house of Judas look for a man of Tarsus
       named Saul..."
    d. **Ananias** answered, "Lord, I have heard from many
       about this man, how much evil he has done..."

In languages that use a developmental marker, this marker is likely to
be used in connection with a change of direction in a reported conversation. It is normal, also, for a noun to refer to the speaker of such a speech,
even when a pronoun would otherwise be expected (see chapter 17).

In languages which group reported speeches into adjacency pairs, the
way a countering move is introduced typically identifies it as *beginning* a
pair rather than ending the one opened by the previous question or other
initiative. In such a language, the exchange of (75) might be reported as in
(76), with (76d) beginning a new adjacency pair.

(76)   a. The Lord said to him in a vision, "Ananias." (IM)
      b. "Here I am, Lord," **he replied.** (RM)
      c. The Lord said to him, "Rise and go to the street called
        Straight, and at the house of Judas look for a man of Tarsus
        named Saul..." (IM)
      d. Ananias **said,** "Lord, I have heard from many about this
        man, how much evil he has done..." (CM/IM)

Key Concepts:

speech orienter

closed conversation

presentation of reported speech

  direct speech

  indirect speech

  semidirect speech

    logophoric pronoun

type of information of reported conversations

adjacency pair

  question-answer

  remark-evaluation

  proposal-implementation

countering move

15

Conventionalized Aspects of Text Organization

Just as expectation structures (e.g., schemata, section 9.4) are conventionalized ways to organize things on the cognitive level, there are other conventions that deal specifically with the organization of texts as linguistic products. In this chapter we consider conventionalized aspects of narratives.

Conventionalized aspects of text organization can either be universal or specific to a particular language and culture. There is a third possibility: conventions can cut across linguistic and cultural boundaries but vary according to genre (chapter 2) or along the oral versus written dimension (chapter 4). All these possibilities are illustrated in this chapter. Research in this area, however, is still in the exploratory stage.

15.1 The story schema

Brewer (1985) uses the term STORY SCHEMA to mean a conventionalized template for organizing the content of narrative.[65] For "fully-formed" oral narratives of personal experience, Labov (1972:363) furnishes the following schema:

- abstract
- orientation
- complicating action

---

[65]Longacre (1996:34) uses the term *anatomy of plot,* and adds, "something like plot characterizes forms of discourse other than narrative".

- evaluation
- result or resolution
- coda

It is possible to have "complex chainings and embeddings of these elements" (loc. cit.), and it is also possible to find narratives which do not have them all. The different parts are now discussed in turn.

15.1.1 Abstract. The term "abstract" includes two kinds of elements: title or abstract proper, and opening (Brewer 1985) or aperture (Longacre 1996:34).

Sometimes stories have a TITLE, an initial expression (often less than a full sentence) by which the story is known. Somewhat the same function is served by an ABSTRACT in the sense of Labov (loc. cit.): "one or two clauses summarizing the whole story". An example from Ayoré of Bolivia is found in Grimes 1975:266: 'I killed a jaguar on another occasion'. Titles are, of course, common in written traditions, but it is not known how common titles and abstracts are in oral traditions.

"Conventionalized story OPENINGS", on the other hand, "occur throughout the world" (Brewer 1985:179), although they are genre specific. Western oral tradition has *Once upon a time* for fairy tales and *Did you hear the one about...* for jokes; the Clackamas Indians of the American Northwest use 'He lived there' as a conventional opening which includes setting information (Thompson 1977:457, cited in Brewer 1985:179). In some languages, openings can be "so formulaic that they have no other meaning; for example, the Zuni story opening is said to be untranslatable" (Tedlock 1972:123, cited in Brewer 1985:179). In written traditions, however, conventionalized openings are generally not found (Brewer 1985:184).

15.1.2 Orientation. An ORIENTATION section is a conventionalized place for setting information (time, place, or circumstances) and for participant introduction (section 12.3). Lines 1–3 of appendix A constitute an orientation section. In oral traditions, there is commonly an orientation section, at least for some genres. As to written traditions, "in more recent [Western] fiction it has become conventionalized to omit the initial setting [i.e., orientation section] and distribute the information throughout the discourse" (p. 185).

15.1.3 Complicating action. The COMPLICATING ACTION or BUILD-UP is a sequence of events leading up to a result or resolution. It has universal status, although exceptions can be found. In appendix A, lines 4–23 can be thought of as a section of complicating action.

15.1.4 Evaluation. EVALUATION as a kind of information was discussed in section 12.3. It gives the point of the text, what the speaker feels about it, and can be expressed either directly (the narrator speaking as him or herself) or indirectly (participants' speech and actions reflecting the narrator's feelings). In the present connection, we ask whether a heavy dose of evaluation occurs conventionally at a certain point in a text. Labov (1972:368ff) found that, in oral narratives of personal experience in the Black inner city, it is very common for evaluation to occur conspicuously before the resolution, although not always as a separate thematic grouping. This happens as well in appendix A, lines 21–22: *Pattie felt his body being pulled away and gripped with all her strength. I'm not giving up my kids, she vowed.* Such evaluation stops the action, makes the hearer wait for the resolution (see 15.1.5), and evokes emotional reaction. "When this is done artfully...the resolution comes with much greater force" (p. 374). Even though there may be a conventional evaluation section in a story schema, evaluation usually occurs in other places as well.

15.1.5 Result or resolution. The RESULT or RESOLUTION section terminates the complicating action. It answers the question, "So what finally happened?" Virtually all folktales are claimed to include some form of conflict resolution (Fischer 1963:237). The term "resolution", however, does not necessarily mean "happy ending". Not only is it becoming more common for stories with "bad" endings to occur in written traditions, but "a number of stories from oral traditions have 'bad' endings from the point of view of a Western reader" (Brewer 1985:183ff). Rather than being a "happy ending", resolution is one which reaffirms a world view, happy or not.

Within the resolution, it is often possible to identify a CLIMAX for the story. This is "the event or point of greatest intensity or interest; a culmination or apex" *(Oxford English Dictionary).* Immediately prior to the climax, it is common to find one or more devices whose rhetorical effect is to slow down the story and create the expectation that the climax is about to be presented. These include the introduction of background information such as an evaluation (see above) and "tail-head linkage" (section 4.1).[66]

Another part of the resolution that may be identifiable is the DENOUEMENT (from French 'untying'), an event section leading down from the peak that spells out the final outcome (Longacre 1996:37). In appendix A, lines 24–28 are denouement.

---

[66]This definition of *climax* differs from that of Hwang (1997:301), for whom the notional climax is "the highest tension point of the story". See Levinsohn 2000:197 for a list of devices associated with climax in Koiné Greek.

15.1.6 Coda. A CODA or EPILOGUE is a final nonevent section "that makes a meta-comment on the story, gives a summary, or gives some post-resolution information about the characters" (Brewer 1985:183), e.g., *And they lived happily ever after.* A coda can also furnish explanation after the fact (as in appendix A, line 29: *Belly-crawling clear of the garage before it disintegrated, Jim had hooked his muscular arms around the base of a pine tree*); it can draw an application (moral) or give a final word of evaluation. Codas are conventionalized in many oral traditions; Brewer (loc. cit.) describes conventionalized codas with different combinations of elements in Clackamas, Limba, Shoshone, Hanga, and Sherpa. Although it is not in vogue in Western written stories to provide explicit morals or summaries, "there is some use of epilogues to give additional information about the course of events after the resolution of the basic conflict" (p. 186).

A CLOSING or FINIS is an expression, generally conventional, indicating the end of the story. In oral traditions, "conventional closings occur very widely" (p. 183). Not only are there simple closings (such as 'That's all' in Mbyá Guaraní), but there are complex and colorful ones, such as "May you become rich in vermin in your provision-shed, but I in cows in my cattle-kraal" (Finnegan 1970:380, cited in Brewer, loc. cit.). Western written texts used to have *The end* as a conventional closing, but that is now rare (p. 186).

You will have noticed that certain natural associations hold between types of information in narrative (chapter 12) and parts of a story schema:

- setting and participant introduction in an orientation section;
- events in sections of complicating action and resolution;
- evaluation in an evaluation section; and
- summary information in an abstract or coda.

A story schema can be expected to reflect productive patterns of foreground and background information, and in some cases there may be no reason to believe that a story schema per se is being imposed. In other cases, regularity of patterning may indicate that the grounding patterns have become conventionalized.

15.2 Patterns of repetition

Besides an overall story schema, certain other aspects of stories can become conventionalized. Stories in oral traditions often show characteristic PATTERNS OF REPETITION. Brewer writes (p. 181),

A very common characteristic of oral traditions is the repetition of character types (e.g., three brothers, three monsters).

The number of repetitions varies from culture to culture. It is five for the Clackamas of the Pacific Northwest (Jacobs 1959:224); it is four for the Navaho (Toelken 1981:167), and it is three for stories in the Western oral tradition such as "The Three Bears" (Olrik 1965 (1909):133).

There can be repetition of episode types as well as of character types: "the protagonist will carry out one act, then a second similar act" (p. 182). It appears that many patterns of repetition in oral traditions are conventionalized.

15.3 Convention in oral and written traditions

Stories from oral traditions also tend to have more conventionalized openings and closings than stories from written traditions. Why? Brewer (p. 189) suggests that an oral narrator may need to indicate a sharp distinction between the text and ordinary conversation; there is no book cover to provide this signal. Some story openings make this distinction explicit, as this one from Ashanti: "We do not really mean, we do not really mean [that what we are going to say is true]" (Rattray 1969:55).

Conventional patterns of repetition in oral traditions can possibly be explained in that they aid in the narrator's fluency or reduce the speaker's (and hearer's) memory load (Brewer 1985:189f). Much the same could be said for story schemata in general.

Regardless of their origin or rationale, conventionalized aspects of discourse organization can be thought of as furnishing a kind of template or outline. When a hearer recognizes one in a text, he or she quickly uses it, in a top-down fashion, to structure the mental representation; subsequent material is easily accommodated. Hearers predictably make use of all available shortcuts in constructing a mental representation.

Key Concepts:
story schema
    title or abstract
    opening
    orientation
    complicating action or build-up
    evaluation
    result or resolution
        climax
        denouement
    coda or epilogue
    closing or finis
patterns of repetition
convention in oral and written traditions

Chapters 16–18

Participant Reference

16

Basic Notions of Reference

There are two reasons why we need to know how participants and other entities are referred to throughout a discourse. First of all, a hearer (or analyst) needs to be able to understand who is doing what to whom. Secondly, a producer of discourse needs to be able to make the same kind information clear to the hearers or readers. The task is not a simple one, since languages have different patterns of reference. The good news is that all such patterns reflect familiar patterns of cognition and discourse organization.

In this chapter and the next, you will learn the basic possibilities for patterns of reference in narrative. From narrative, it should be possible to extend your understanding to other genres.

16.1 Linguistic devices for reference

Givón (1983:18) provides a well-known scale of devices that are used in languages for reference:

(77) Scale of coding weight for referring expressions

Most Coding Material   full noun phrases
                        stressed/independent pronouns
                        unstressed/bound pronouns ("agreement")
Least Coding Material   zero anaphora

111

Here, ZERO ANAPHORA refers to lack of any explicit referring device, even agreement. Example (77) can be thought of as a scale of linguistic salience which matches up in an iconic way with informational salience, according to the general principle that linguistic salience increases with informational salience (Givón, loc. cit. and 1990:969). Before we examine what that means in specific cases, we take note of differences among languages in relation to (77).

Languages differ in what referring devices are available with lower coding weight than full noun phrases.

- Isolating languages, of course, have little or no agreement; other languages have verb agreement with up to three arguments.
- So-called "pro-drop" languages commonly do without free arguments (another sense in which the term zero anaphora is used), whereas free arguments are the norm in languages like English.
- Languages vary greatly in categories of information carried by pronouns and agreement. Some systems signal only person; others signal person, number, gender or noun class, honorific status, etc.

What this means is that the specific levels in (77) are not the same in all languages. Still, each language will have its own version of such a scale, and the same generalizations will hold.

16.2 What systems of reference must do

A viable system of reference in any language must accomplish three kinds of tasks.

(78)   Three tasks of a scheme of reference

Semantic	identify the referents unambiguously, distinguishing them from other possible ones
Discourse-pragmatic	signal the activation status and prominence of the referents or the actions they perform
Processing	overcome disruptions in the flow of information

Concerning the SEMANTIC TASK, explicitness in identification is a relative notion: very rarely are referents identified in a completely explicit way. In appendix A, Pattie Uridel is identified by first and last name when she is introduced. Subsequently, she is referred to as *Pattie, she, her, his slightly built wife,* etc. The object is not to distinguish the referent from all other theoretically possible ones (many people in the world are named Pattie), but rather from other *practically* possible ones. The hearer will scan his or her current mental representation for possible referents of a given expression and will settle on the one which best fits with what is being said (i.e., in terms of the schema or other expectation structures; see section 9.4). Predictably, when there is more than one plausible referent in a given context, the identifying expression will be more specific.[67] In general, the semantic part of the referring task predicts that *the amount of coding material in a referring expression increases with the danger of ambiguity.* Often, the hearer needs "hard data" on only one of the arguments in a clause; then, with that one identified and with the aid of selectional restrictions and contextual clues, the others can be identified.

In regard to the DISCOURSE-PRAGMATIC TASK in (78), the amount of coding material in a reference varies with the referent's status in activation or prominence: *the higher the activation status, the less coding material is necessary* (section 10.1). In terminology traditional in narrative analysis, participants are spoken of as being "introduced", "kept on stage", and "dismissed"; after they have been dismissed, they may at some point be "reintroduced" or "brought back on stage". Using the more general terms from section 10.1, we can say that participants are activated (or reactivated), maintained in active status, and deactivated (Chafe 1987; see Givón 1990:915). Activation is commonly accomplished with a full noun phrase. If the participant will be prominent in the text, an initial activating noun phrase is often prominent as well in discourse-pragmatic structuring: such a noun phrase is often the focus and may even appear in a presentational configuration (see (42) in chapter 11). Maintaining a participant in active status requires only minimal coding (agreement or pronouns). Deactivation is often done without formal means (see the deactivation of Pattie's husband, Jim, in appendix A, lines 7–12). This means that the participant central to the story (section 17.2.1), once activated, will typically require only minimum coding, whereas referents of short-term significance (hence many props) may have full descriptive noun phrases.

In regard to the PROCESSING TASK, *more coding material is generally needed whenever the flow of information is disrupted.* Disruptions in narrative occur at breaks in thematic continuity (i.e., at boundaries of thematic groupings—chapter 7) and possibly when there is a change in type of information (e.g., from event material to nonevent material—chapter 12).[68] At such places, coding for reference generally increases.

---

[67]There are usually not more than three participants active at any one point in a narrative (Grimes 1975:261, 269).

Thus, the three tasks of a system of reference (semantics, discourse-pragmatics, processing) all illustrate the iconic principle presented in connection with (77).

Givón (1983:141–214) notes that the choice of referring expression in Ute depends on where it occurs in its thematic grouping: initial, medial, or final. The following pattern holds in Ute when the subject of successive sentences remains the same.

(79)   Ute referring expressions with subject continuity

初期 initial position: full noun phrase
medial position: zero
final position: independent pronoun

This pattern is consistent with the referential tasks we have just described. Following a disruption in the flow of information at the boundary of a thematic grouping, participant updating commonly occurs, so it is not surprising to find full noun phrases there (section 7.4). As participants are maintained in active status in the middle of a thematic grouping, minimal coding is employed. The slight increase in coding weight final in the grouping reflects the increase in prominence commonly given to events that realize the goal of the grouping. Consequently, a pattern similar to that found in thematic groupings in Ute is normal, cross-linguistically.

Fox (1987:168) notes for English that "full NP's are used to demarcate new narrative units". She cites the following example (p. 169).

(80)   ...She was in at least ten, maybe twenty fathoms of water. Then what was she standing on? For, there was no question that she was standing on something. She drained water from her mask and put her face down and saw that the manta had come beneath her and had risen, like a balloon, until it rested just at her feet.
   Did it want something? Was it injured again? **Paloma** took a breath and knelt on the manta's...
   (Peter Benchley, *The Girl of the Sea of Cortez*, p. 226)

In the above passage, the name *Paloma* is used at the first mention of the participant in the new paragraph, even though the pronoun *she* would not have been more ambiguous there than in the preceding text.

---

[68]However, see Fox 1987:163f for some cases when switching kinds of information apparently does not affect the pattern of reference.

Key Concepts:
scale of coding weight
   zero anaphora
three tasks of a scheme of reference
   semantic
   discourse-pragmatic
   processing

17

Strategies of Reference

In chapter 16, we considered linguistic devices available in a system of reference and what they must do. In this chapter, we consider how the task of reference in discourse is actually done. We consider two types of STRATEGIES of reference: sequential (look-back) strategies and VIP strategies.[69] Though all languages probably use both, the extent to which they prefer one over the other appears to vary considerably.

17.1 Sequential (look-back) strategies

There are different kinds of sequential or look-back strategies, but they have three things in common. First, they are basically concerned with how to identify the referent of expressions that are lower than full noun phrases on the coding scale (77). Second, as implied by the term *look-back* (Givón 1983:13), these strategies identify the referent of such expressions by noting what or who was mentioned most recently (perhaps restricted to a certain category, such as subject). Third, sequential strategies make no reference to discourse organization (Fox 1987:158).

In a SEQUENTIAL STRATEGY, "the reference of [other than a full noun phrase] is normally taken from the nearest candidate word before it" (Grimes 1978:viii). By "candidate word" or phrase is meant an antecedent that agrees with the reference in relevant categories (e.g., number, gender), that has an animacy category appropriate in that proposition, and that is plausible in terms of the current expectation structure.

---

[69]This basic opposition is due to Grimes (1978:vii–viii). What we are calling a VIP strategy, he calls a "thematic strategy".

SUBJECT-ORIENTED SEQUENTIAL STRATEGIES typically work as follows: to find the referent of a main clause subject, look back to the subject of the preceding (main) clause. Consider the sample passage in (81).

(81)   "The Hare and the Dog" with subject-oriented sequential strategy.

     a. One day **the hare** went and talked with the dog.
     b. **He** told the dog, "Fry one of your pups for us to eat!"
     c. **The dog** refused.
     d. **The hare** asked **him,** "Why won't you fry it?"
     e. **The dog** answered, "...."

In a sequential strategy, all participants, such as the dog and the hare in (81), follow the same rule.

English makes some use of a subject-oriented sequential strategy, according to Fox (1987:162, 170f). Unless other factors intervene, a subject pronoun refers to the subject of the preceding clause (if the gender is right).

(82)   Before Vader could gather his thoughts much further,
     though, Luke attacked again—much more aggressively. **He**
     advanced in a flurry of lunges....
             (James Kahn. 1983. *Return of the Jedi,* p. 156)

In (82), the bolded pronoun refers to Luke. When the subject changes, a noun phrase must be used.

(83)   When Vader moved to parry, Luke feinted and cut low.
     Vader counterparried...
             (op. cit., 154)

Fox claims that sequential strategies account for a high percentage of the available cross-linguistic data on reference (pp. 158f).[70] However, she rejects them as a comprehensive description of reference because they disregard discourse structure and have too many exceptions. Tomlin's (1987:456) criticism is similar.

---

[70]Fox (1987:158) sums up Givón 1983 as follows: "In an impressive collection of data from several unrelated languages, pronouns are shown to be used when the distance to the last mention of the referent is small (and there are no interfering referents), while full NPs are shown to be used when that distance is somewhat great (and/or if there are interfering referents)."

17.2 VIP strategies

In a VIP (VERY IMPORTANT PARTICIPANT) STRATEGY, "one referent is distinguished from the rest when introduced, and a special set of terms refer to it no matter how many other things have been mentioned more recently" (Grimes 1978:viii). One way to recast "The Dog and the Hare" with a VIP strategy would be as in (84), with the dog as VIP and X representing some linguistic signal of that fact.

(84) "The Hare and the Dog" with VIP strategy

      a. One day the hare went and talked with **the dog-X.**
      b. The hare told **X,** "Fry one of your pups for us to eat! "
      c. **X** refused.
      d. The hare asked **X,** "Why won't you fry it?"
      e. **X** answered, "…"

A VIP can be identified either on the global level (for the text as a whole), or on a local level (for a particular thematic grouping). For whatever level a participant is VIP, that part of the text is in some sense about that participant: that part of the mental representation will be linked to the VIP in a special way. This structuring of the mental representation will typically involve linguistic signals and not just some idea of prominence. Here, as elsewhere, we are concerned with linguistic patterns; these normally turn out to be indicators of content-based categories.

17.2.1 Major and minor participants, global VIPs. Just as certain languages make a distinction between primary and secondary events (section 12.2), some have different patterns of reference on the global level for major and minor participants (neither category includes props). Notionally, MAJOR PARTICIPANTS are those which are active for a large part of the narrative and play leading roles; minor participants are activated briefly and lapse into deactivation. Major participants typically have a different overall pattern of reference and a different way of being introduced.

Major participants commonly have a formal introduction, whereas minor participants do not. A FORMAL INTRODUCTION is linguistic material that instructs the hearer not only to activate the participant, but also to be prepared to organize a major part of the mental representation around him or her. This prominence can be signaled either on the level of the proposition (through presentational or other nonactive sentences) or on the level of the concept (e.g., with a special indefiniteness marker).

A presentational sentence (section 11.2) is structured so that the new referent is focal, typically following a verb of existence. Thus, an entire proposition is used to activate the entity and establish its special status: participants thus introduced usually figure prominently in what is to follow.

(85) Mbyá Guaraní

     a. *Yma   je   o-iko mokoi ava-kue*
        long.ago hearsay 3-be two   man-COLL
        Long ago there lived two men.

     b. *Ha'e kuery ma   je   o-mba'e-apo   petei jurua*
        3.ANA COLL   boundary hearsay 3-thing-make one   non.Indian

        pe
        DAT
        They worked together for a certain non-Indian.

The presentational sentence (85a) is followed by one (85b) in which the newly introduced referent is a topic, making immediate and prominent use of the newly-established node in the mental representation.

    Nonactive sentences with verbs like 'have' can be used like presentationals to introduce major participants.

(86) Koiné Greek (Luke 15:11)

     anthro:pos tis   eichen   duo huios
     man   certain 3SG.had two sons
     A certain man had two sons.

Example (86) has topic-comment articulation, with the sons having the focus as they are introduced.

    Recall that an indefinite referent is one for which the speaker is instructing the hearer to create a slot or node in his or her mental representation (section 10.2). Many languages have ways to signal indefiniteness which indicate, in addition, that the new entity is to occupy a prominent place. For example, it is common in languages for a special indefinite determiner "one, a certain" to be used in the introduction of major participants (Hopper and Thompson 1984:719). This is the case with *petei* 'one' in (85b) and *tis* 'a certain' in (86).

When a major participant is already well known to the hearers, however, there is often no need for formal introduction.

(87) Mbyá Guaraní
      nhande-ru   tenonde   yvy   o-nhono
      1+2-father   in.front earth   3-lay
      Our original father established the earth.

Among the major participants, patterns of reference sometimes make it necessary to recognize one as GLOBAL VIP.[71] After being introduced, the global VIP is often referred to by minimum, but virtually constant, coding. In Mambila, the global VIP, once introduced, is referred to by zero (when subject) or the third person singular pronoun *bú* (Perrin 1978:110).

(88) a. *neye   woh tohtoh da,   heh tull **bú***
         person take bird   that give put to.him
         The person took that bird and gave it to him.

      b. ∅ *ndi ka   eh   seh*
            go still with it
         He went off with it.

      c. ∅ *nda baneh   a   mi   neye   deh   a*
            go particle locative house person certain direction
         He went to the house of a certain person.

      d. *mun a   neye   dehne whe dehneneh*
         child possessive person sit   cry continuous
         The person's child was sitting crying.

      e. ∅ *jia me   a ndia "…"*
            say mother to thus
         He said to the mother, "…"

      f. *me   jia **bú** a, "…"*
         mother say him   to
         The mother said to him, "…"

---

[71]In this treatment, the assumption is that there will be no more than one global VIP per text. Sometimes the global VIP is called the *central character;* however, sometimes "central characters" are so designated because of their prominent role in the plot, not because of a particular strategy for reference, as are VIPs in our sense.

g. Ø *jia ma*   *a* "..."
    say mother to
    He said to the mother, "..."

Whereas "the main participant [our "global VIP"] is identified as little as possible once he is introduced..., participants other than the main one are
re-identified by a noun every time they are mentioned" (with certain exceptions; p. 110f). Thus, 'mother' is referred to by a noun phrase throughout
(88).

Sometimes the global VIP has its own special pronoun, but that is not as
common.

MINOR PARTICIPANTS are generally introduced with full noun phrases but
without formal introduction. Often, they are active for only part of the
narrative.

17.2.2 Local VIPs. Even when a text does not have a global VIP, individual thematic groupings can have a LOCAL VIP. This participant is sometimes called the thematic participant (Grimes 1975) for that grouping. His
or her thematic status can be indicated in a variety of ways, two of which
are illustrated below.

One way is for the local VIP to be topic, or grammatical subject, in virtually every sentence. Sometimes, this requires the use of passivization or
some other valence-changing operation. In some of the Arawá languages
of Brazil, the thematic participant is regularly the topic or PIVOT.[72] The
prefix represented by 'Ø-' indicates that the object is the pivot.

(89) "The Hare and the Dog" adapted to an Arawá language

    a. One day hare went and talked with **dog**.
    b. Hare Ø-told, "Fry one of your pups for us to eat!" he
        said.
    c. Ø refused.
    d. Hare Ø-asked, "Why don't you fry it?" he said.
    e. Ø answered, "..."

In (89), dog's local VIP status is shown by its being the pivot and referred
to by zero throughout 2–5.

---

[72]When marking within the clause (generally on the verb) confers on one particular
grammatical relation a privileged syntactic status, that grammatical relation is called the
(syntactic) pivot; see Van Valin 1993:56ff.

Another way to distinguish the local VIP from other participants, found in a number of African languages, is for the local VIP to be the only activated participant that does NOT take a determiner.

(90) "The Hare and the Dog" adapted to Kaba (Central African Republic)

  a. One day that hare went-and-talked with **dog.**
  b. He said, "Fry one of your pups for us to eat!"
  c. That-time **dog** refused.
  d. That-time that hare asked, "Why don't you fry it? "
  e. That-time **dog** answered, "..."

We note here four final observations about local VIPs:

- If a narrative as a whole has a global VIP as well as local VIPs, the global VIP will typically *not* be a local VIP, even in sections where he or she is "on stage".
- Use of local VIPs can be partial; that is, some thematic groupings may have local VIP, while others follow a sequential strategy.
- At the climax of a narrative, all or none of the major participants may be marked as local VIPs.[73]
- Local VIPs may be limited largely to oral texts.

The concept of a local VIP readily fits into the broader category of CENTER OF ATTENTION. In English, there is evidence that, among active concepts, only one is at the center of attention at any given time. Linde (1979) claims that only this centrally active entity (if neutral in gender) can be referred to by the pronoun *it.* Consider (91) and (92), both taken from descriptions of apartments.

(91) And the living room was a very very small room with two windows that wouldn't open and things like that. And **it** looked nice. **It** had a beautiful brick wall.

(92) You entered into a tiny hallway and the kitchen was off **that.**

Linde claims that *it* can be used (twice) in (91) because it refers to the entity at the center of attention (the living room). *That,* however, is used in (92) to refer to the hallway because, by the time it occurs, the speaker has already shifted the center of attention to the kitchen. Although the fine

---

[73]In such instances, a sequential strategy is perhaps being employed, with heavy referential coding for the purpose of prominence.

points of this kind of analysis doubtless can use further study, note that *that* cannot be used in place of *it* in ((91); nor can *it* be used in place of *that* in (92), without awkwardness, even though the hallway is still active by any standard.

17.3 Describing systems of reference

In a given language, one or both of the reference strategies presented in this chapter will interact with the basic requirements for reference mentioned in section 16.2, and complexity often results. A useful way of describing this involves two levels: the default case and special cases:

- the DEFAULT CASE is the pattern which holds when there is no great discontinuity, surprise, etc.;
- SPECIAL CASES are patterns which come into play when there are discontinuities, surprises, or other complexities.

This format, involving rule ordering, makes it possible to handle a large number of variables. In many languages, the default case seems to be some type of sequential strategy, with VIP strategies as special cases. This would account for the gross statistical correctness of sequential strategies mentioned by Fox (1987:159), while dealing with exceptions to that norm and taking other factors into account.

A description of subject coding in this format is illustrated for English in (93); see section 18.2 for a description for Mofu-Gudur of Cameroon.

(93)   English subject coding for narrative, simplified (Fox 1987)

Default case
- If subject is the same as in preceding clause, use pronoun.

Special cases
- At the beginning of a thematic unit, use full NP.
- others...

Strategies of reference vary with the language, and within a language can vary with genre, individual style, and medium of production (oral versus written), that is, with text types discussed in chapters 1–4. Chapter 18 provides a methodology for analyzing patterns of reference.

Key Concepts:
 strategies for reference
  sequential (look-back) strategies
  VIP strategies
    global strategies
      major and minor participants
      global VIP
    local strategies
      local VIPs
      center of attention
  default case/special case description

18

A Methodology for Analyzing Reference Patterns

The more certain we are of the law, the more clearly we know that if new factors have been introduced, the result will vary accordingly. C. S. Lewis, *Miracles*

This chapter describes a methodology for identifying the different factors that affect the amount of coding material that is used when a speaker refers to participants throughout a discourse. The methodology involves eight steps.[74]

18.1 Draw up an inventory of ways of encoding references to participants

Make a list of the different ways in which reference to a participant can be made in the language. Typically, these ways may be grouped into four categories or amounts of coding material similar to those listed in Givón's scale of coding weight for referring expressions (section 16.1).

The text in Mofu-Gudur of Cameroon that is used to illustrate the points of this chapter (see (94) below) employs all four categories: zero (the absence of a noun phrase, represented by ——); unstressed pronouns (hereafter referred to as verb prefixes and suffixes); stressed pronouns (represented by

---

[74]This chapter largely follows Levinsohn 1994:112–120, though steps 4 and 5 have been modified.

PN); and nouns with or without qualifiers.[75] The verb prefix is obligatory, and indicates whether the subject is singular (3s) or plural (3p). It is not attached to ideophones, however.

18.2 Prepare a chart of participant encoding in a text

Start analyzing participant reference with a third-person text of the type described in section 8.1. The chart should have separate columns for displaying how references to subjects and non-subjects are encoded.

The chart in (94) has five columns. Following a narrow column which gives the sentence reference (Ref) is an optional column which notes the intersentential connectives (Conn) and interclausal spacers (SP; see section 11.7) used in the text. The next two columns indicate the encoding of subjects and non-subjects, respectively, using the categories of section 18.1 (the significance of the bracketed numbers is explained in section 18.3). When the only reference to a non-subject is a verb suffix, this is noted in the non-subject column. The final column provides a free translation (abbreviated, as appropriate) of the remainder of each clause. This includes the contents of reported speeches, since these are embedded in the overall structure of the narrative. Ideophones are signaled by an exclamation mark after the gloss.

(94)

Ref	Conn	Subject	Non-subject	Free translation
1		stranger [1]		3s-be.
2a		wife the [2]		3s-not find something;
2b		PN [1]		3s-not find something.
3	next	hunger	(suffix) [1]	3s-strike-3s.
4a	then	—— [1]		3s-go
4b		—— [1]		3s-journey.
5a		—— [1]		3s-go
5b	SP	—— [1]	children sitting [3]	3s-perceive.
6		—— [1]	(suffix) [3]	3s-say-to.3p, "What are you doing?" "We are sitting here guarding,"
7		children [3]	(suffix) [1]	3p-answer-3s like this.
8		—— [1]	—— [3]	—— "What are you guarding?"
9		—— [3]	—— [1]	—— "Sheep and goats."

[75]See Pohlig and Levinsohn 1994 for the function of the qualifiers. The chart of section 2 does not indicate when the qualifier that marks the referent as locally salient is present.

Ref	Conn	Subject	Non-subject	Free translation
10		—— [3]	stranger the [1]	3p-answer, "Are you a thief?"
11a		—— [1]	—— [3]	—— " Would I steal from children?
11b				You there, how do you wipe your hands?"
12		child [3a]	—— [1]	3s-say, "I wipe them like this."
13		—— [1]		—— "You there, is it that way at your home, too?"
14a		child [3b]	—— [1]	3s-say, "I wipe them like this,"
14b		—— [3b]		gesturing like a deaf-mute.
15		stranger [1]		3s-say, "You there, how do you wipe your hands?"
16		—— [3c]	—— [1]	—— "My father gives me soap."
17		stranger [1]	to child the [3c]	3s-say, "Let's go to your home!"
18	then	—— [1/3c]	with child the [3c]	3p-go to their house.
19a		—— [1/3c]		3p-go to their house
19b	SP	man that [4]	goat [5]	slaughter! 3s-slaughter.
20		—— [4]		3s-say, "A stranger has come."
21	then	woman that [6]	(verb suffix) [1/4] meat this [5]	3s-prepare-for.3p
22	then	—— [1/4/6?]	(verb suffix) [5]	3p-eat-3s
23		stranger [1]		3s-say, "Please give me the foot!"
24		woman that [6]	to husband the [4]	—— "Give it him, then!"
25		husband the [4]	(verb suffix) [6]	3s-say-to.3s, "How can I give him only a foot?"
26		woman that [6]		3s-say, "I'm going to the river."
27		husband the [4]	for stranger [1]	stand up! to go 3s-look for something.
28a		stranger SP [1]	into kitchen	tiptoe! enter!
28b		—— [1]	foot [5a]	3s-steal.
29a		—— [1]	foot [5a]	3s-steal
29b		—— [1]	(verb suffix) [5a]	3s-crunch-3s
29c	SP	husband of woman that [4]		return!
29d		woman that [6]	from river	return!
30	next	shame	(verb suffix) [4/6]	3s-fill-3p

Ref	Conn	Subject	Non-subject	Free translation
31		stranger [1]	(verb suffix) [4/6]	3s-say-to.3p, "Just leave me the foot...!"
32		story the		3s-finished.

18.3 Track the participants

Allocate a number to each participant that is referred to more than once in the text. On the chart, label references to participants (including zero).

In the chart of the Mofu-Gudur text (94), the numbers used to denote the participants are as follows: [1] the stranger; [2] his wife; [3] the children; [3a], [3b], [3c] individual children; [4] the children's father; [5] the goat/meat; [5a] the cooked foot of the goat; and [6] the children's mother.

18.4 Identify the context in which each reference to a participant occurs

First of all, identify the context for each *activated subject* in the text. For each clause or sentence, identify which of the following contexts is applicable:

(95) S1 the subject is the same as in the previous clause or sentence
      S2 the subject was the addressee of a speech reported in the previous sentence (in a closed conversation—chapter 14)
      S3 the subject was involved in the previous sentence in a non-subject role other than in a closed conversation
      S4 other changes of subject than those covered by S2 and S3

These four contexts are illustrated in (96), using English sentences based on the Mofu-Gudur text (94). The subject reference that fits the context concerned is bolded.

(96) S1 The stranger entered the kitchen. **He** stole the foot.
      S2 The boys asked the stranger, "Are you a thief?" **He** replied...
      S3 Hunger afflicted the stranger. **He** went to look for food.
      S4 Then shame filled them. **The stranger** said to them...

Typically, context S1 extends also to situations in which the subject and non-subject of the previous sentence combine to form a single, plural subject. In the following extract (97), for example, *they* refers to the stranger plus the boy. Languages typically treat such contexts as instances of 'same subject'.

(97)   S1   The stranger said to the boy, "Let's go to your house!" **They** went.

To each activated subject of the text, allocate the label S1, S2, S3, or S4, according to the context in which it is found. For example, the subjects of the first seven sentences of the Mofu-Gudur text (94) would be allocated the labels in (98) (INTRO means the participant is being introduced or activated for the first time).

(98)   1   INTRO
       2a   INTRO
       2b   S4
       3   INTRO
       4a   S3
       4b–6   S1
       7   S2

Now, identify the context for each activated *non-subject* in the text. For each clause or sentence, identify which of the following contexts is applicable:

(99)   N1   the referent occupies the same non-subject role as in the previous clause or sentence
       N2   the addressee of a reported speech was the subject (speaker) of a speech reported in the previous sentence
       N3   the referent was involved in the previous sentence in a different role than that covered by N2
       N4   other non-subject references than those covered by N1–N3

The four contexts in (99) are illustrated in (100), using English sentences based on the Mofu-Gudur text (94). The reference that fits the context concerned is given in caps.

(100) N1   He stole the foot. When he stole the **foot**...
       N2   He said to them...The children answered **him**...

N3 Then shame filled them. The stranger said to **them...**

N4 The stranger said, "Give me the foot!" The woman
said to **her husband...**

To each activated non-subject of the text, allocate the label N1, N2, N3, or N4, according to the context in which it is found. For example, the non-subjects of the first ten sentences of the Mofu-Gudur text would be allocated the following labels:

(101) 3   N3
       5b   INTRO
       6   N3
       7–9   N2
       10   N1

18.5 Propose default encodings for each context

Based on either a statistical count or an inspection of the data, propose a default encoding for each of the contexts identified in section 18.4.

In the Mofu-Gudur text, provisional default encodings for subjects might be as in (102) (NP indicates a noun, with or without qualifiers, together with the obligatory verb prefix—see section 18.1).

(102) S1 zero (with ideophones)
          verb prefix (elsewhere)
      S2 NP
      S3 NP[76]
      S4 NP

Default encodings for non-subjects in Mofu-Gudur are not considered in this chapter.

18.6 Inspect the text for other than default encoding

Label each reference to a participant in the text as to whether the material used is or is not the default encoding for the context. If it is not the default encoding, distinguish whether the amount is less than or more than the default encoding.

---

[76]The only example of context S3 in the text is clause 4a, the encoding of which is a verb prefix. Typically, though, the default encoding for S3 is never less than that proposed for S2.

For example, the clauses and sentences from the Mofu-Gudur text that are considered in (98) would be labeled as follows for the amount of coding material used for activated subjects:

(103) 2b   S4: less than default
      4a   S3: less than default
      4b–6 S1: default
      7   S2: default

The amount of coding material in clause 2b is less than default because the default encoding for context S4 is a noun (phrase), but only a pronoun is used. The same is true for clause 4a; the default encoding for context S3 is a noun (phrase), but only a verb prefix is used.

We now consider reasons why the amount of coding material might be less or more than predicted.

18.6.1 When the coding material is less than predicted. When encoding is less than the default amount, this is typically because the referent is a VIP (section 17.2); there is only one major participant on stage, or a cycle of events is being repeated.

In the Mofu-Gudur text (94), less than the proposed default amount of coding material for subject occurs in clauses 2b and 4a (see (103)). In addition, no speech orienter is used in sentences 8, 9, 11, 13, and 16, even though the default encoding for context S2 is a noun (phrase).

Less than the default amount of coding material may have been used in clauses 2b and 4a because the referent is a VIP and no other major participant is on stage (the stranger's wife appears no further in the story). As for the sentences without a speech orienter, two types of conversation may be distinguished.

- Sentences 6–11a describe a closed conversation (chapter 14) between a stranger and a group of children and, once the participants have been established, a speech orienter is used only when there is a change in the direction of the conversation (sentence 7). The fact that the verb prefixes of Mofu-Gudur distinguish singular and plural assists in the identification of the participants.

- The speeches reported in sentences 11b–16, however, consist of three parallel adjacency pairs (chapter 1 and section 14.2), each involving the stranger and a different child. Since all the speakers are individuals, the prefixes attached to the verb do not assist in identification. Speech orienters are omitted only in sentences 13 and 16. Further examples of this type of repeated pattern would be needed in order to determine why these particular orienters, rather than others, were omitted.

18.6.2 When the coding material is more than predicted. A similar procedure to that described in section 18.6.1 is followed for instances in which encoding is greater than the default amount proposed. Increased encoding typically occurs immediately following points of discontinuity and in connection with information highlighting (Levinsohn 2000:140).

The following extract from another Mofu-Gudur text illustrates increased coding material in context S1 (the same subject as in the previous sentence). In Mofu-Gudur, the default encoding for context S1 is a verb prefix only (section 18.5). The initial adverbial phrase *one day* indicates that sentence b occurs immediately following a discontinuity of time, hence the motivation for the increased coding material.

(104) a. After that, ——[chief] 3s-put-3s [bird] in its place.
      b. One day, chief   3s-left   for field.

18.7 Incorporate any modifications to the proposals of section 18.5

Once you determine the factors that are involved when encoding is more or less than predicted, you may need to modify the list of contexts for which default encodings are proposed. For example, if the amount of coding material for context S3 were frequently less than the default amount proposed, the default encoding might be modified to give different amounts according to the number of participants on stage. An example might be, "If a non-subject in one clause becomes the subject of the next and a major participant is interacting with a minor participant or is alone..."

18.8 Generalize the motivations for deviances from default encoding

Having eliminated all references that may be interpreted as instances of default encoding, the remaining deviations are judged to be special forms of encoding. Determine the motivation for each instance of special encoding, and draw generalizations. As indicated in section 18.6, common motivations for increased encoding include the presence of a discontinuity and the highlighting of information, while decreased encoding is typically used to identify a VIP.

> **Key Concepts:**
> inventory of ways of encoding references to participants
> chart of participant encoding
> tracking participants
> identifying the context for each reference to a participant
> proposing default encodings for defined contexts
> inspecting the text for other than default encoding
>   less than the predicted amount
>   more than the predicted amount
> modifying the proposals for default encodings
> generalizing the motivations for special encodings

Appendix A

"Winds of Terror"

Written text by Peter Michelmore
(Reprinted with permission from the February 1991 Reader's
Digest. Copyright 1991 by The Reader's Digest Assn., Inc.[77])

1 The afternoon sky was darkening by the minute as Pattie Uridel, 36, drove home from her job as an insurance executive in Aurora, Ill.

2 Black clouds were sweeping in from the northwest, separated from the fields of ripening corn and beans by only a pale ribbon of light.

3 *You could jump up and touch them,* she thought.

4 Then came the downpour.

5 Hailstones as big as golf balls hammered her car as she pulled into her driveway in the Wheatland Plains subdivision, nine miles southeast of Aurora.

6 Birch trees bent horizontally in the wind.

7 She considered staying in the car, but the garage door opened and the husky figure of her husband, Jim, appeared.

8 Jim, who'd been stowing away patio furniture, liked to call his slightly built wife Toughie, because of her energy and determination.

9 Pattie parked the car and made for the kitchen door.

---

[77]The numbered sentences concern the effect of the tornado on the Uridel family, and reference is made to a number of them in the body of this manual. The unnumbered sentences concern other aspects of the storm. We include them because Reader's Digest requires that we reproduce the article in its entirety.

10 Three of the four Uridel children—Kathryn, four, Alex, eight, and Gregory, nine—came running when Pattie entered the kitchen.
11 Jimmy, ten, was visiting friends.
12 "Let's go downstairs," she said urgently, leading them to the family room in the basement.
13 Suddenly the room went black.
14 Then came the sound of shattering glass and groaning timber.
15 Pattie swept the children into her arms as the roof shot from the house and the walls blew down.
16 Mother and children clung desperately to one another, pounded by rain and flying furniture.
17 "What do you call this?" Kathryn cried out in terror.
18 "Tornado!" Pattie screamed.
19 Shards of glass cut her arms, and a piece of lumber glanced off the back of her head.
20 "Mom!" cried Gregory. "I can't hold on!"
21 Pattie felt his body being pulled away and gripped with all her strength.
22 *I'm not giving up my kids,* she vowed.

Death and Destruction. Meteorologists at the National Severe Storms Forecast Center in Kansas City, Mo., had issued a severe-thunderstorm watch for the region that Tuesday afternoon, August 28, 1990, but had not foreseen a tornado. Instead of dissipating as expected as it moved to the southeast, the storm grew stronger. Then at its core, amid powerful counterclockwise winds and updrafts pushing 60,000 feet above the earth, the tornado was born. Curtained by the deluge of rain and hail, the twister's funnel first struck three small buildings in Oswego, south of Aurora. By now the twister had reached F2 on the tornado scale—significant but not the most severe. The most powerful tornadoes ever confirmed have been F5s.

This one was widening rapidly, spawning a cluster of smaller twisters. Inside the hydra-headed monster winds built to an estimated 250 m.p.h.

By the time the tornado crossed into Will County, it was approaching an F5, so powerful it stripped bark from trees and gouged the very earth from the fields. Ahead of it lay a string of housing subdivisions and the city of Joliet.

23 For 30 seconds, Pattie and the children held fast.
24 Then the tornado passed, and climbing from the basement, they saw twisted sheets of siding, roof sections and battered cars everywhere.
25 A man stumbled toward them, blood pouring from a lacerated ear.
26 "Dad!" the kids shouted.
27 Tearfully, Pattie embraced Jim.
28 "We thought you were dead," she said.
29 Belly-crawling clear of the garage before it disintegrated, Jim had hooked his muscular arms around the base of a pine tree.

Though more than 60 houses had been damaged or destroyed in Wheatland Plains, and many residents had been injured, no one was killed. But just a few miles south, the tornado crossed U.S. Highway and hurled three drivers in their cars to their death. A fourth would tell of sitting behind the wheel with his seat belt fastened one moment and standing on the road the next.

Drawing Breath. At the high school in Plainfield (pop. 4,000), coaches ordered football players indoors. The first slam of wind, at 3:35, killed the lights, and the athletes retreated into a hallway behind the gym. Girl volleyball players jammed in after the boys.

"Cover your heads!" shouted football coach Wayne DeSutter, 46, whose own sons, Kevin, 16, and Adam, 11, were in the hallway. One of the seniors took off his helmet and put it on Adam.

Doors shot open, ceiling lights crashed down, debris whizzed through the air. Hearing a loud *whoosh*, DeSutter looked up. The gym ceiling and three walls had collapsed. Only the hallway remained intact.

Although two custodians and a teacher were killed, incredibly all of the 150 athletes and coaches were safe. Had the tornado struck 24 hours later, the potential for death would have been enormous: 1,000 students were returning after summer break.

Evidence would show that the storm briefly eased after destroying the school. But the beast was only drawing breath. A mile farther along, its winds were again at full force, leveling everything in its path.

In Naperville, Eileen Glaser and co-workers at a medical research center were warned at 3:30 not to leave the building because of high winds.

There was no word of any tornado, but Eileen felt uneasy about her sons Ryan, 15, and Josh, 11, who were at the family home in Crystal Lawns, south of Plainfield.

Ryan delivered the Joliet *Herald-News* and Josh often helped. Usually, the boys started about 4 p.m.

Eileen dialed home, intent on telling the boys to postpone delivery. No one answered. Ryan, a musician in the school band, had decided to deliver his papers early because he had a church youth-group meeting that evening.

He and Josh were on opposite sides of the street when the sky blackened. "Deliver your papers and run home as fast as you can," Ryan shouted to his brother.

Josh had gone only a few yards before hail and wind chased him into a garage. Grabbing a corner post, he felt his legs being swept straight out behind him. Then the garage began to break apart. Josh let go of the post and crawled away, blood streaming from his scalp.

At last able to stand, Josh dodged through the clutter in the street. "Ryan!" he called. "Ryan!" There was no answer. He ran home, where neighbor Jerry Sullivan found him. Sullivan and another neighbor went out to look for Ryan. They found him lying in a pile of broken lumber. "My back hurts," said Ryan, stirring to consciousness.

The hard edge of a piece of timber was protruding between the boy's shoulder blades. One man cradled Ryan in his arms while the other ran to find an ambulance.

"It's not good," said a surgeon to John and Eileen Glaser at the St. Joseph Medical Center that evening. A one-foot length of lumber had become embedded in Ryan's back, piercing a lung and his heart. Eileen dropped to her knees in prayer. Some time later the surgeon came to say that Ryan had died.

"Let Me Down." At St. Joseph, the injured arrived on foot and by car as well as by ambulance. One was Arthur Jagos, 32, a Will County sheriff's deputy. Jagos had awakened to the sound of hail outside his home in Joliet. His wife, Suzanne, and two young children were away. Clambering out of bed, he began closing the upstairs windows. To his horror, he felt his feet lift off the floor.

Fetal position, his brain told him. Shutting his eyes, he rolled his six-foot-two-inch, 190-pound body into a tight ball. He was aware of the house disintegrating, the rain drenching his back and his body spinning in the funnel. "Oh, my God!" he cried. He saw boards and beams flying with him. *Don't torture me,* he thought. *Let me down or kill me.*

He was thrown against a pile of construction dirt, 300 feet from his home. The pain in his chest was unbearable, but Jagos surged with a will to live. *My kids are going to have a father,* he swore.

Struggling free of debris, he staggered forward. Doctors who treated him later found his heart and lungs bruised, his legs bloodied and his back stripped of skin, but he would recover.

Others were not as fortunate. Police and firefighters found the body of a 12-year-old boy in a cornfield beside a parking lot. Looking farther, they came upon the bodies of a young woman and an infant. Eight bodies would be found in the vicinity, the people sucked from their brick apartment complex and thrown 60 yards to their death in the field.

Here at last, at the edge of Joliet, the tornado stopped its murderous rampage and curled back into the thunderstorm, which blew itself out over Indiana.

Cruelly, ten minutes after the monster hit, the weather service issued its first tornado warning for Will County, and the civil-defense siren finally wailed in Joliet.

The tornado killed 28 people and injured over 350. Along its 16-mile path, two schools and close to 500 homes were destroyed. Damage amounted to over $200 million, including cleanup and rebuilding expenses.

In the subdivision where Ryan Glaser was struck down, the housing loss was put at 63. Here, as elsewhere, volunteers poured in by the hundreds to help. Families were rebuilding by the fall, and some hoped to be in new homes by Christmas.

The sadness in this community over Ryan's death has been profound, but spirits have been buoyed by the strength of his devoutly Catholic mother. "God love those people who helped Ryan that afternoon," Eileen Glaser says. "I feel like the Lord made sure he was with friends."

Eileen has encouraged her three surviving children to talk of their terror and grief, so that they can get on with living.

The slender, sandy-haired boy who asked to take over Ryan's newspaper route understands the lesson. His name is Josh Glaser.

Appendix B

"The Train Ride"

(Unedited oral text by Patricia Olson (Olson 1992:71f))

(Pauses of greater than one second are indicated numerically; minor pauses are indicated by punctuation.)

1 When the one year we were going to come to Omaha for Christmas.
2 And we thought that since the roads are often very icy that it might be safer and wiser if we took the train,
3 and then we wouldn't have to worry about road conditions.
4 So, we got on a lovely train in Duluth.
5 It was really nice, and we thought, "Oh, boy, this is going to be fun.
6 Fun for us and fun for the four kids." (2.1)
7 And then we got off in Minneapolis where we had to change trains.
8 And when it was time to get on the next train, we got in line. (2.5)
9 And then nothing happened.
10 We stood there, and stood there.
11 And finally, they told us, "The train is late."
12 "Well, when will the next train be leaving?"
13 "Oh, maybe in a couple hours." (1.2)
14 So, in a couple hours we got back in line again, waiting to get on the train, with zillions of other people.
15 But, again, they announced the train will be later.
16 "Why is the train going to be later?"
17 "The train is going to be later because they don't have an engine.

18 We have to find an engine before we can move this train out of here." (1.4)
19 So after waiting another two hours, it was finally announced, "Train for Omaha will be leaving in so many minutes."
20 So again we hustled everybody together and gathered all our packages and started for the train.
21 Only, because we had all these little children trying to get to the train, were moving slower than other people. (1.2)
22 And so by the time we got to the train, there were no seats left on the one and only coach.
23 "Now what do we do?"
24 They had a solution.
25 They had an empty boxcar, or mail car I guess it was, that um didn't have any seats in it.
26 But if we wanted to go on the train, we could go on the train and sit on the floor.
27 Which we decided we would do since we wanted to get to Omaha and not stay in Minneapolis all night in the train station.
28 And that worked pretty well because sitting on the floor, the kids could lay down on the floor and go to sleep.
29 And it was probably more comfortable than sitting in a seat for them. (1.7)
30 But then as day broke, we came into the middle of Iowa.
31 And uh-oh, the train stops.
32 "What's the problem?"
33 "Oh, there's been a train derailment up ahead.
34 We can't get through.
35 We have to stop here for hours and hours." (2.0)
36 Well, since our little train was a little bit primitive with one passenger car and the rest were boxcars, um there was nothing to eat of course.
37 And with four little children and two of them not even a year old yet, it was a little hectic.
38 And they were a little hungry. (1.3)
39 So we could see off in the distance that there was a little town.
40 But for some strange reason, I was the only one that had boots.
41 So we plodded off across the field to this little town, to try and find some food for the people on the train.
42 There were a few other people that went with, but I led the way because I had my boots.

43 So we found a little bit of grub, not too much in that little town because about all they had there was a bar.

44 And they didn't have too much on hand that we could eat. (2.7)

45 So then we came back to the train, and after about six hours, we finally got moving again.

46 We had gone a short distance, maybe less than a hundred miles, and we came to a railroad crossing.

47 And guess what—the train hit a car. (1.0)

48 Another slight delay happened.

49 And so we sat there until all that was taken care of and cleared away.

50 And we arrived into Omaha, finally 24 hours after we were supposed to have been there, spending all this time on the train.

51 Which we could have driven and probably been a lot safer and a lot more comfortable. (1.0)

52 But it was an experience that we will not soon forget.

53 And, it really caused our desire to ride on trains to disappear once and for all. (2.8)

54 To add to this dilemma and frustration, we had to go back on the train since we didn't have a car.

55 So we decided to switch to another railroad line which maybe would be a little bit more...up to date.

56 Well, the train was up to date.

57 But again they didn't have enough room.

58 So instead of sitting in a boxcar, we got to sit on our suitcases on the way home, from Omaha to Minneapolis.

59 About halfway there, there was some nice couple that decided to let us sit in the, or share their seat.

60 And so we took turns sitting on suitcases and sitting on the seat.

61 Because with the little kids it was rather difficult to sit on the suitcases. (1.7)

62 And then when we finally got to Minneapolis, and we're thinking, "Oh boy, now maybe we can get on the nice train from Minneapolis to Duluth."

63 We got on one that probably went back to the 1880s that looked like an old street car. (1.8)

64 So once again we were disappointed and had a very reluctant—oh, reluctant isn't the right word—we had a very disappointing ride on a train.

65 And to say the least, we never rode the train in the United States again.

Appendix C

Extract from "The Healer and His Wife"

Oral text extract from the Tyap language of Nigeria
(see Follingstad 1994:155, 165–166)

In the following extract, *kàn* is the developmental marker, while *kìn* and *ma* are additives (see chapter 13 and below). These markers occur between the subject and the verb.[78] The sentences are numbered, with individual clauses given letters.

Before the extract starts, introductory sentences have told about the healer, his wife Bashila, their having a child, her not knowing that he used to go and eat people, his looking after the child while she was away grinding, and his keeping the child quiet by singing to it, while entertaining it with a necklace he had made from his victims' fingernails.

1a	Bashila was coming from grinding,		
		she	*kàn* heard the healer singing to their child [that he used to go and eat people]

---

[78]A further particle, the foreground marker *si,* also occurs between the subject and the verb in several clauses of this extract—loc. cit.

145

1b		she		stood behind the room
1c		she		heard the song that he was singing.
2a		Bashila	kìn	passed
2b–d		she		entered, she returned, she kept quiet.
3a		He		took the child
3b		he		gave it to Bashila.
4	It became morning,	he		got up, he got up.
5	When he got up,	he		left, he again went to eat people.
6a	When he went to eat people,	Bashila	ma kàn	got up
6b		she	kìn	gathered her things
6c		she		fetched ashes
6d		she		added an egg
6e		she		put the things on her head
6f		she		caught the road.
7a	She caught the road, she went, she went, she went,			
		she	kàn	looked
7b		she		saw the healer.
8		Healer	ma kàn	saw her.
9		Healer		said, 'What kind of woman looks like this?'
10a	He walked, he walked, he walked, the woman was nearing him,			
		she	kàn	rubbed the ashes on her face
10b		she	kàn	put the egg in her mouth.
11a	She reached him,	she	kàn	bit down on the egg
11b		she		bit down on it in her mouth
11c		the egg	kàn	burst [all over her face].
12a	There	he		said that the woman was not his wife,
12b				that she could pass.
13		The woman	kìn	passed.

Observations

Neither *kàn* nor *kìn* is used during the introductory sentences. The first time *kàn* is used is in connection with the event that changes Bashila's attitude to her husband: while returning from grinding, she overhears what he is singing, and thereby discovers that he is a cannibal (sentence 1). The next developments in the story are found in sentences 6, 7, and 8–9. Then, as the climax of this extract is reached, each individual act in the woman's disguise is marked as a new development (sentences 10–11).

In sentence 6, *kàn* marks the whole of the sentence as a new development. The story will develop through Bashila's actions, not those of her husband, but the significant development is not her getting up (6a—something she does every day), but the events of the rest of the sentence. These events are appended to 6a by the additive *kìn.*

Two functions of *kìn* are illustrated in this passage: confirmation (the healer tells the woman she can pass + she does so—sentences 12–13), and appending information of unequal importance. In the case of sentences 1–2, the information appended by *kìn* is less important than what she overheard. In sentence 6, however, the information appended by *kìn* is of great importance.

References

Aaron, Uche E. 1998. Discourse factors in Bible translation: A discourse manifesto revisited. Notes on Translation 12:1–12.

Adams, Marilyn Jager, and Allan Collins. 1979. A schema-theoretic view of reading. In New directions in discourse processing, ed. by Roy O. Freedle, 1–22. Norwood, N.J.: Ablex.

Aissen, Judith L. 1992. Topic and focus in Mayan. Language 68:43–80.

Anderson, Stephen R., and Edward Keenan. 1985. Deixis. In Language typology and syntactic description, ed. by Timothy Shopen, vol. 3, 259–308. Cambridge: Cambridge University Press.

Andrews, Avery. 1985. The major functions of the noun phrase. In Language typology and syntactic description, ed. by Timothy Shopen, vol. 1, 62–154. Cambridge: Cambridge University Press.

Bakhtin, M. M. 1986. The problem of speech genres. In Speech genres and other late essays, ed. by M. M. Bakhtin, 60–102. Austin: University of Texas Press.

Barnes, Janet. 1984. Evidentials in the Tuyuca verb. International Journal of American Linguistics 50:255–271.

Bartsch, Carla. 1997. Oral style, written style, and Bible translation. Notes on Translation 11:41–48.

Beekman, John, John Callow, and Michael Kopesec. 1981. The semantic structure of written communication, fifth ed. Dallas, Tex.: Summer Institute of Linguistics.

Beneš, Eduard. 1962. Die Verbstellung im Deutschen, von der Mitteilungsperspektive her betrachtet. Phonologica Pragensia 5:6–19.

Biber, Douglas. 1988. Variation across speech and writing. Cambridge: Cambridge University Press.

Blakemore, Diane. 1987. Semantic constraints on relevance. Oxford: Blackwell.

Blakemore, Diane. 1992. Understanding utterances: An introduction to pragmatics. Oxford: Blackwell.

Blass, Regina. 1990. Relevance relations in discourse: A study with special reference to Sissala. Cambridge: Cambridge University Press.

Blass, Regina. 1993. Constraints on relevance in Koiné Greek in the Pauline letters. Nairobi: Summer Institute of Linguistics, Exegetical Seminar, May 29–June 19, 1993.

Bolinger, Dwight L. 1952. Linear modification. Publication of the Modern Language Association of America 67:1117–1144.

Bolinger, Dwight L. 1977. Another glance at main clause phenomena. Language 53:11–19.

Brewer, William F. 1985. The story schema: Universal and culture-specific properties. In Literacy, language, and learning: The nature and consequences of reading and writing, ed. by David R. Olson, Nancy Torrance, and Angela Hildyard, 167–194. Cambridge: Cambridge University Press.

Brown, Gillian, and George Yule. 1983. Discourse analysis. Cambridge: Cambridge University Press.

Callow, Kathleen. 1974. Discourse considerations in translating the Word of God. Grand Rapids: Zondervan.

Chafe, Wallace L. 1976. Givenness, contrastiveness, definiteness, subjects, topics, and point of view. In Subject and topic, ed. by Charles N. Li, 25–56. New York: Academic Press.

Chafe, Wallace L. 1980. The deployment of consciousness in narrative. In The pear stories: cognitive, cultural, and linguistic aspects of narrative production, ed. by Wallace L. Chafe, 9–50. Norwood, N.J.: Ablex.

Chafe, Wallace L. 1985a. Information flow in Seneca and English. Proceedings of the Eleventh Annual Meeting of the Berkeley Linguistics Society, 14–24.

Chafe, Wallace L. 1985b. Linguistic differences produced by differences between speaking and writing. In Literacy, language, and learning: the nature and consequences of reading and writing, ed. by David R. Olson, Nancy Torrance, and Angela Hildyard, 105–123. Cambridge: Cambridge University Press.

Chafe, Wallace L. 1987. Cognitive constraints on information flow. In Coherence and grounding in discourse, ed. by Russell S. Tomlin, 21–51. Amsterdam: John Benjamins.

Chafe, Wallace L. 1991. Discourse: an overview. In International Encyclopedia of Linguistics, ed. by William Bright, 1:356–358. New York: Oxford University Press.

Chafe, Wallace L. 1992. The flow of ideas in a sample of written language. In Discourse description: Diverse linguistic analyses of a
fund-raising text, ed. by William C. Mann and Sandra A. Thompson,
267–294. Amsterdam: John Benjamins.

Chomsky, Noam. 1971. Deep structure, surface structure, and semantic
representation. In Semantics, ed. by Danny D. Steinberg and Leon A.
Jakobovits, 183–216. Cambridge: Cambridge University Press.

Comrie, Bernard. 1989. Language universals and linguistic typology,
second ed. Chicago: University of Chicago Press.

Coulthard, Malcolm. 1977. An introduction to discourse analysis. London: Longman.

Crozier, David H. 1984. A study in the discourse grammar of Cishingini.
Ph.D. dissertation. University of Ibadan, Nigeria.

Crystal, David. 1997. A dictionary of linguistics and phonetics, fourth
ed. Oxford: Blackwell.

Cruttenden, Alan. 1986. Intonation. Cambridge: Cambridge University
Press.

Dayley, Jon. 1985. Tzutujil grammar. Berkeley: University of California
Press.

de Beaugrande, Robert. 1997. The story of discourse analysis. In Discourse
studies: A multidisciplinary introduction. vol. 1: Discourse as structure
and process, ed. by Teun A. van Dijk, 35–62. London: Sage.

de Beaugrande, Robert, and Wolfgang U. Dressler. 1981. Introduction to
text linguistics. London: Longman.

DeLancey, Scott. 1987. Transitivity in grammar and discourse. In Coherence and grounding in discourse, ed. by Russell S. Tomlin, 53–68.
Amsterdam: John Benjamins.

Derbyshire, Desmond C. 1985. Hixkaryana and linguistic typology. Summer Institute of Linguistics and the University of Texas at Arlington,
Publications in Linguistics 75. Dallas.

Dik, Simon. 1978. Functional grammar. Amsterdam: North-Holland.

Dik, Simon, Maria E. Hoffman, Jan R. de Jong, Sie Ing Djiang, Harry
Stroomer, and Lourens de Vries. 1981. On the typology of focus
phenomenon. In Perspectives on functional grammar, ed. by Teun
Hoekstra, Harry van der Hulst, and Michael Moortgat, 41–74.
Dordrecht: Foris.

Dooley, Robert A. 1982. Options in the pragmatic structuring of Guaraní
sentences. Language 58:307–31.

Dooley, Robert A. 1990. The positioning of non-pronominal clitics and particles in lowland South American languages. In Amazonian linguistics: Studies in lowland South American languages, ed. by Doris L. Payne, 457–483. Austin: University of Texas Press.

Dry, Helen Aristar. 1992. Foregrounding: an assessment. In Language in context: Essays for Robert E. Longacre, ed. by Shin Ja J. Hwang and William R. Merrifield, 435–450. Summer Institute of Linguistics and the University of Texas at Arlington Publications in Linguistics 107. Dallas.

Dryer, Matthew. 1992. The Greenbergian word order correlations. Language 68:81–138.

Eggins, Suzanne and J. R. Martin. 1997. Genres and registers of discourse. In Discourse studies: A multidisciplinary introduction, vol. 1: Discourse as structure and process, ed. by Teun A. van Dijk, 230–256. London: Sage.

Everett, Daniel L. 1992. Formal linguistics and field work. Notes on Linguistics 57:11–25.

Fillmore, Charles J. 1981. Pragmatics and the description of discourse. In Radical pragmatics, ed. by Peter Cole, 143–66. New York: Academic Press.

Finnegan, Ruth. 1970. Oral literature in Africa. Oxford: Clarendon Press.

Firbas, Jan. 1964. From comparative word-order studies. BRNO studies in English 4:111–126.

Fischer, J. L. 1963. The sociopsychological analysis of folktales. Current Anthropology 4:235–295.

Follingstad, Carl M. 1994. Thematic development and prominence in Tyap discourse. In Discourse features in ten languages of West-Central Africa, ed. by Stephen H. Levinsohn, 151–190. Summer Institute of Linguistics and the University of Texas at Arlington Publications in Linguistics 119. Dallas.

Fox, Barbara A. 1987. Anaphora in popular written English narratives. In Coherence and grounding in discourse, ed. by Russell S. Tomlin, 157–174. Amsterdam: John Benjamins.

Frank, Lynn. 1983. Characteristic features of oral and written modes of language: Additional bibliography. Notes on Linguistics 25:34–37.

Garvin, Paul L. 1963. Czechoslovakia. In Current trends in linguistics, ed. by Thomas A. Sebeok, 1.499–522. The Hague: Mouton.

Givón, Talmy. 1982. Logic versus pragmatics, with human language as the referee: Toward an empirically viable epistemology. Journal of Pragmatics 6:81–133.

Givón, Talmy, ed. 1983. Topic continuity in discourse. Amsterdam: John Benjamins.

Givón, Talmy. 1984/90. Syntax: A functional-typological introduction. 2 vols. Amsterdam: John Benjamins.

Graesser, Arthur C., Morton A. Gernsbacher, and Susan R. Goldman. 1997. Cognition. In Discourse studies: A multidisciplinary introduction, vol. 1: Discourse as structure and process, ed. by Teun A. van Dijk, 292–319. London: Sage.

Green, Georgia M. 1976. Main clause phenomena in subordinate clauses. Language 52:382–397.

Greenberg, Joseph H. 1963. Some universals of grammar with particular reference to the order of meaningful elements. In Universals of language, ed. by Joseph H. Greenberg, 73–113. Cambridge, Mass.: MIT.

Grimes, Joseph E. 1975. The Thread of discourse. The Hague: Mouton.

Grimes, Joseph E., ed. 1978. Papers on discourse. SIL Publication No. 51. Dallas: Summer Institute of Linguistics.

Gundel, Jeanette K. 1988. Universals of topic-comment structure. In Studies in syntactic typology, ed. by Michael Hammond, Edith A. Moravcsik, and Jessica R. Wirth, 209–39. Amsterdam: John Benjamins.

Halliday, M. A. K. 1978. Language as social semiotic: The social interpretation of language and meaning. London: Edward Arnold and Baltimore: University Park Press.

Halliday, M. A. K., and Ruqaiya Hasan. 1976. Cohesion in English. London: Longman.

Healey, Phyllis, and Alan Healey. 1990. Greek circumstantial participles tracking participants with participants in the Greek New Testament. Occasional Papers in Translation and Textlinguistics 4:173–259.

Hobbs, Jerry. 1985. On the coherence and structure of discourse. Center for the Study of Language and Information, Stanford University, Technical Report CSLI-85-37.

Hopper, Paul J., ed. 1982. Tense-aspect: Between semantics and pragmatics. Amsterdam: John Benjamins.

Hopper, Paul J. and Sandra A. Thompson. 1980. Transitivity in grammar and discourse. Language 56:251–299.

Hopper, Paul J. and Sandra A. Thompson. 1984. The discourse basis for lexical categories in universal grammar. Language 60:703–752.

Howell, James F., and Dean Memering. 1986. Brief handbook for writers. Englewood Cliffs, N.J.: Prentice-Hall.

Huisman, Roberta D. 1973. Angaataha narrative discourse. Linguistics 110:29–42.

Hwang, Shin Ja J. 1997. A profile and discourse analysis of an English short story. Language Research 33:293–320.

Jackendoff, Ray S. 1972. Semantic interpretation in Generative Grammar. Cambridge, Mass.: MIT Press.

Jacobs, Melville. 1959. The content and style of oral literature: Clackamas Chinook myths and tales. Chicago: University of Chicago Press.

Johnson-Laird, P. N. 1983. Mental models. Cambridge, Mass.: Harvard University Press.

Johnston, Ray. 1976. Devising a written style in an unwritten language. Read 11:66–70.

Labov, William. 1972. Language in the inner city: Studies in the Black English vernacular. Philadelphia: University of Pennsylvania Press.

Lakoff, George. 1972. Hedges: A study in meaning criteria and the logic of fuzzy concepts. Papers from the Eighth Regional Meeting of the Chicago Linguistics Society, 183–228.

Lambrecht, Knud. 1994. Information structure and sentence form: Topic, focus, and the mental representation of discourse referents. New York: Cambridge University Press.

Larson, Mildred L. 1984. Meaning-based translation: A guide to cross-language equivalence. Lanham, Md.: University Press of America.

Leech, Geoffrey N. 1983. Principles of pragmatics. London: Longman.

Levinsohn, Stephen H. 1976. Progression and digression in Inga (Quechuan) discourse. Forum Linguisticum 1:122–147.

Levinsohn, Stephen H. 1992. Preposed and postposed adverbials in English. 1992 Work Papers of the Summer Institute of Linguistics, University of North Dakota Session 36:19–31.

Levinsohn, Stephen H. 1994. Field procedures for the analysis of participant reference in a monologue discourse. In Discourse features in ten languages of West-Central Africa, ed. by Stephen H. Levinsohn, 109–121. Summer Institute of Linguistics and the University of Texas at Arlington Publications in Linguistics 119. Dallas.

Levinsohn, Stephen H. 1999. Ordering of propositions in OV languages in Brazil. Notes on Translation 13(1):54–56.

Levinsohn, Stephen H. 2000. Discourse features of New Testament Greek: A coursebook on the information structure of New Testament Greek, second ed. Dallas: SIL International.

Li, Charles N. 1986. Direct speech and indirect speech: A functional study. In Direct and indirect speech, ed. by F. Coulmas, 29–45. Mouton de Gruyter.

Li, Charles N., and Sandra A. Thompson. 1976. Subject and topic: A new typology of language. In Subject and topic, ed. by Charles N. Li, 457–489. New York: Academic Press.

Linde, Charlotte. 1979. Focus of attention and the choice of pronouns in discourse. In Syntax and semantics, vol. 12: Discourse and syntax, ed. by Talmy Givón, 337–354. New York: Academic Press.

Longacre, Robert E. 1985. Sentences as combinations of clauses. In Language typology and syntactic description, ed. by Timothy Shopen, 2:235–286. Cambridge: Cambridge University Press.

Longacre, Robert E. 1996. The grammar of discourse, second ed. New York: Plenum.

Longacre, Robert E., and Stephen H. Levinsohn. 1978. Field analysis of discourse. In Current trends in textlinguistics, ed. by Wolfgang U. Dressler, 103–122. Berlin: De Gruyter.

Lyons, John. 1977. Semantics. 2 vols. Cambridge: Cambridge University Press.

MacWhinney, Brian. 1991. Processing: Universals. In International Encyclopedia of Linguistics, ed. by William Bright, vol. 3, 276–278. New York: Oxford University Press.

Mann, William C., and Sandra A. Thompson. 1987. Rhetorical Structure Theory: A theory of text organization. In The structure of discourse, ed. by Livia Polanyi. Norwood, N.J.: Ablex. (Reprinted (1987) as report ISI/RS-87-190, Marina del Rey, CA: Information Sciences Institute, from which citations are taken. Reduced version published (1988) as Rhetorical Structure Theory: toward a functional theory of text organization. Text 8:243–281.)

Mfonyam, Joseph Ngwa. 1994. Prominence in Bafut: Syntactic and pragmatic devices. In Discourse features in ten languages of West-Central Africa, ed. by Stephen H. Levinsohn, 191–210. Summer Institute of Linguistics and the University of Texas at Arlington Publications in Linguistics 119. Dallas.

Mithun, Marianne. 1987. Is basic word order universal? In Coherence and grounding in discourse, ed. by Russell S. Tomlin, 281–328. Amsterdam: John Benjamins. (Revised version in Pragmatics of word order flexibility, ed. by Doris L. Payne, 15–61. Amsterdam: John Benjamins.)

Nida, Eugene A. 1967. Linguistic dimensions of literacy and literature. In World literacy manual, ed. by Floyd Shacklock, 142–161. New York: Committee on World Literacy and Christian Literature.

Nuyts, Jan. 1991. Aspects of a cognitive-pragmatic theory of language; on cognition, functionalism, and grammar. Amsterdam: John Benjamins.

Ochs, Elinor. 1997. Narrative. In Discourse studies: A multidisciplinary introduction, vol. 1: Discourse as structure and process, ed. by Teun A. van Dijk, 185–207. London: Sage.

Olrik, Axel. 1965. Epic laws of folk narrative. In The study of folklore, ed. by Alan Dundes. Englewood Cliffs, N.J.: Prentice-Hall. Translated from original German version, 1909.

Olson, Daniel. 1992. A comparison of thematic paragraph analysis and vocabulary management profiles for an oral corpus. M.A. thesis. University of North Dakota.

Paivio, Allan, and Ian Begg. 1981. Psychology of language. Englewood Cliffs, N.J.: Prentice-Hall.

Palmer, F. R. 1986. Mood and modality. Cambridge: Cambridge University Press.

Payne, Doris L., ed. 1992. Pragmatics of word order flexibility. Amsterdam: John Benjamins.

Pederson, Eric, and Jan Nuyts. 1997. Overview: On the relationship between language and conceptualization. In Language and conceptualization, ed. by Jan Nuyts and Eric Pederson, 1–12. Cambridge: Cambridge University Press.

Perrin, Mona. 1974. Direct and indirect speech in Mambila. Journal of Linguistics 10:27–37.

Perrin, Mona. 1978. Who's who in Mambila folk stories. In Papers on discourse, ed. by Joseph E. Grimes, 105–118. Dallas: Summer Institute of Linguistics.

Perrin, Mona. 1994. Rheme and focus in Mambila. In Discourse features in ten languages of West-Central Africa, ed. by Stephen H. Levinsohn, 231–241. Summer Institute of Linguistics and the University of Texas at Arlington Publications in Linguistics 119. Dallas.

Pike, Kenneth L., and Evelyn G. Pike. 1982. Grammatical analysis, second ed. Dallas, Tex.: Summer Institute of Linguistics and University of Texas at Arlington.

Pohlig, James N., and Stephen H. Levinsohn. 1994. Demonstrative adjectives in Mofu-Gudur folktales. In Discourse features in ten languages of West-Central Africa, ed. by Stephen H. Levinsohn, 53–90. Summer Institute of Linguistics and the University of Texas at Arlington Publications in Linguistics 119. Dallas.

Radford, Andrew. 1988. Transformational grammar: A first course. Cambridge: Cambridge University Press.

Rattray, R. S. 1969. Akan-Ashanti folk-tales. Oxford: Clarendon Press.

Reinhart, Tanya. 1982. Pragmatics and linguistics: An analysis of sentence topics. Bloomington, Ind.: Indiana University Linguistics Club.

Roberts, John R. 1997. The syntax of discourse structure. Notes on Translation 11(2):15–34.

Sandig, Barbara, and Margret Selting. 1997. Discourse styles. In Discourse studies: A multidisciplinary introduction, vol. 1: Discourse as structure and process, ed. by Teun A. van Dijk, 138–156. London: Sage.

Schank, Roger C., and Robert P. Abelson. 1977. Scripts, plans, goals and understanding. Hillsdale, N.J.: Laurence Erlbaum Associates.

Sperber, Dan, and Deirdre Wilson. 1986. Relevance: communication and cognition. Chicago: University of Chicago Press.

Spielman, Roger. 1981. Conversational analysis and cultural knowledge. Notes on Linguistics 17:7-17.

Spreda, Klaus W. 1994. Notes on markers of parallelism in Meta'. In Discourse features in ten languages of West-Central Africa, ed. by Stephen H. Levinsohn, 223–230. Summer Institute of Linguistics and the University of Texas at Arlington Publications in Linguistics 119. Dallas.

Tannen, Deborah. 1979. What's in a frame? Surface evidence for underlying expectations. In New directions in discourse processing, ed. by Roy O. Freedle, 137–181. Norwood, N.J.: Ablex.

Tedlock, Dennis. 1972. On the translation of style in oral narrative. In Toward new perspectives in folklore, ed. by Americo Paredes and Richard Bauman. Austin: University of Texas Press.

Thompson, Sandra A. 1987. "Subordination" and narrative event structure. In Coherence and grounding in discourse, ed. by Russell S. Tomlin, 435–454. Amsterdam: John Benjamins.

Thompson, Sandra A., and Robert E. Longacre. 1985. Adverbial clauses. In Language typology and syntactic description, ed. by Timothy Shopen, vol. 1, 171–234. Cambridge: Cambridge University Press.

Thompson, Stith. 1977. The folktale. Berkeley: University of California Press.

Toelken, B. 1981. The "pretty languages" of Yellowman: genre, mode, and texture in Navaho coyote narratives. In Folklore genres, ed. by D. Ben-Amos. Austin: University of Texas Press.

Tomlin, Russell S., ed. 1987. Coherence and grounding in discourse. Amsterdam: John Benjamins.

Tomlin, Russell S., Linda Forrest, Ming Ming Pu, and Myung Hee Kim. 1997. Discourse semantics. In Discourse studies: A multidisciplinary introduction, vol. 1: Discourse as structure and process, ed. by Teun A. van Dijk, 63–111. London: Sage.

Tomlin, Russell S., and Richard Rhodes. 1979. An introduction to information distribution in Ojibwa. Papers from the Fifteenth Regional Meeting of the Chicago Linguistics Society, 307–321. Chicago: Chicago Linguistics Society.

van Dijk, Teun A. 1977. Text and context. London: Longman.

van Dijk, ed. 1997. Discourse studies: A multidisciplinary introduction, vol. 1: Discourse as structure and process. London: Sage.

Van Valin, Robert D., Jr. 1993. A synopsis of Role and Reference Grammar. In Advances in Role and Reference Grammar, ed. by Robert D. Van Valin, Jr., 1–164. Amsterdam: John Benjamins.

Watters, John R. 1979. Focus in Aghem: A study of its formal correlates and typology. In Aghem grammatical structure, ed. by L.M. Hyman, 137-97. Southern California Occasional Papers in Linguistics. Los Angeles: UCLA.

Index

Z

8227310R0

Made in the USA
Charleston, SC
19 May 2011